The Mystery of the Menorah

...and the Hebrew Alphabet

By J. R. Church
and Gary Stearman

All scripture references are from the King James Version unless otherwise stated.

The Mystery of the Menorah

. . . and the Hebrew Alphabet

First Edition, 1993

Copyright © 1993 by Prophecy in the News, Inc.

Printed in the United States of America

Published by:

Prophecy Publications

P. O. Box 7000

Oklahoma City, OK 73153

Library of Congress Catalog Card Number 93-84621

ISBN 0-941241-13-0

To Our Jewish Friends

As Christians, we understand that there will be certain differences between us, particularly on the matter of salvation and the identity of the Messiah. But please allow us to express loving support for both Israel and the Jewish people.

The authors, as writers and researchers in biblical prophecy, believe that a great change may lie in the near future for humanity. This change will be of a cataclysmic nature, bringing mankind into the era when the Messiah will arrive to establish His kingdom. As a result of this change, Israel's righteous remnant will be elevated to a special place of prominence in world affairs.

In the ancient past, God the creator, maker of heaven and earth, uttered certain promises to His people through the prophets. We believe that those promises will be kept, because the One who both created His people and spoke to them has a plan that will be brought to pass. In the design of the Menorah and the Hebrew alphabet, that plan may be clearly seen.

We respect your reverence for the Word, and particularly as it applies to a study such as the one we have undertaken in this book.

Our goal is to show Christians that the righteous remnant of Israel has been placed by God in a particular position, ready for the change that lies ahead. Similarly, we wish to show you that our New Testament fits the same pattern that God originated before time began. His ways are higher than our ways, whether we are Christians or Jews.

We thank you and your commentators for your place in the preservation of God's Word. May He soon move upon the face of the earth to produce an era of peace and justice under the Messiah.

Foreword

The concept set forth in this book will give you a renewed appreciation for the divine design of the Bible. Frankly, we must admit that though we are both rooted in mainline theology and have given ourselves to a study of Scripture for many years, we were astounded by the fact that we had never before observed the theme or message contained in this discovery.

Having learned about the strange encoding of the word "Torah" found in Genesis through Deuteronomy, our minds were prepared to make another amazing discovery: the sevens in the Bible correspond to the seven-branched Menorah of the Tabernacle and the Temple. Looking further, we found that the center of each of these menorahs carried the message of the *Ner Elohim,* or "Light of God." No matter where the sevens are encountered in God's word, they carry this pattern. This is particularly true of the Book of Revelation.

When we first saw this amazing truth, we were filled with a sense of God's majesty and perfection. The truth of the Bible's divine inspiration emerged with new meaning. It was early fall, 1992, and we knew we had discovered an important message that begged to be published.

We had hardly dealt with this new truth until

another astounding design came to light. The significance of Revelation's "sevens" brought to mind another pattern. Namely, the 22 chapters of the Bible's final book caused us to think about its possible relationship to the 22 letters of the Hebrew alphabet. Imagine our surprise when we discovered that each of the 22 chapters of Revelation corresponded perfectly with the symbolic meanings of the Hebrew Alphabet!

How did we arrive at this position? Among other sources, we referred to a book entitled, THE WISDOM IN THE HEBREW ALPHABET, by Rabbi Michael L. Munk. For countless centuries, Jewish expositors have taught that each of the letters in their alphabet is a reflection of God's creative power. They believe their alphabet is a manifestation of God's essence and that—taken as a whole—it speaks of His attributes.

We found that the 22 chapters of Revelation bear out this idea. Jesus announces, *"I am Alpha and Omega ..."* in Revelation 1:8. He announces it again in Revelation 22:13. Once one's mind has been opened to the possibility of a connection, it takes little or no imagination to realize that Jesus is telling us He is the alphabet—in the Hebrew, literally the *aleph* and the *tahv* —the opening and closing letters of the Hebrew alphabet. Naturally, this would include all the letters between. It followed then, that in Revelation, each chapter would correspond to its respective Hebrew letter.

At this point, we realized that the message simply had to go out, and with all possible speed. We thought at the time that this was to be a very abbreviated, very slim edition, designed for high impact—to get out a brief statement, and get it out quickly. But in the process of compiling the information, an amazing thing happened. We were suddenly made aware that this message was of such a size and scope that a booklet simply couldn't do it justice.

The expansion began in earnest when we noted that Jews (at the time of Jesus and before) considered their Scriptures to consist of 22 books! Commentators at that time even stated that the 22 books corresponded to the 22 letters of the Hebrew alphabet. We looked at those books and we looked at the Hebrew letters. Again, the correlation matched perfectly! Book by book, the Old Testament, when condensed to its original 22 books, bore out the same symbolic pattern.

Quickly, we made the same investigation of the New Testament. There, of course, we found 27 books, seemingly too many for a match. Too many, that is, until we added the five Hebrew "final letters" to the alphabet. Once again, we discovered a perfect match! And here, we found a special message of finality, or culmination.

Seen as a large-scale structure, and not merely a collection of stories, prophecies and teachings, the Bible commands renewed respect. No longer will it be possible to view it as the mere creation of men, who themselves are mere creations. We, therefore, challenge you to read this book—more than that, study its message and compare it with your view of the Bible. You will emerge with a renewed appreciation of the grandeur of God's design.

Table of Contents

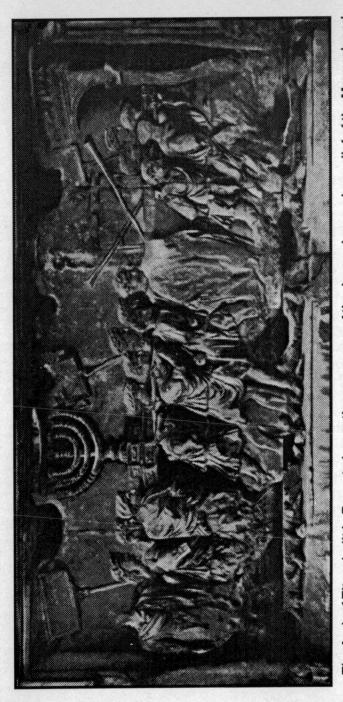

The Arch of Titus, built in Rome to honor the conqueror of the Jews, shows a bas relief of the Menorah and other Temple items carried by Jewish slaves in the parade following the destruction of Jerusalem in AD 70.

Chapter One

The Mystery of the Menorah

What happened to the Menorah, the golden lampstand, that graced the early Tabernacle and the Temple of King Solomon? Can we trace its history? In A.D. 70, The Romans carried the booty of the Jerusalem Temple to Rome. A stone relief of the Temple Menorah can be viewed in the Triumphal Arch of Titus, located just north of the Colosseum in Rome. Edward Gibbon, in his volumous work, THE DECLINE AND FALL OF THE ROMAN EMPIRE, suggested that Herod's Temple Menorah may lie at the bottom of the Mediterranean Sea, somewhere between Italy and the northern coast of Africa.

Gibbon wrote, "At the end of 400 years, the spoils of Jerusalem (the holy instruments of Jewish worship, the gold table and the gold candlestick with seven branches) were transferred from

Rome to Carthage, by a Barbarian ... the haughty Vandal; who immediately hoisted sail, and returned ... to the port of Carthage."[1] However, the twelve ships that carried the loot encountered a storm at sea. We are told that "the vessel which transported the relics of the Capitol was the only one of the whole fleet that suffered shipwreck ... this cargo ... was lost in the sea."[2]

Gibbon indicated that the spoils of the Jewish Temple went down with the ship, including the Menorah. But, was that Menorah the original lampstand built at Sinai? Probably not. According to Jewish historians, it could have been one of Solomon's ten menorahs built to embellish and enhance the Mosaic Menorah which was placed among them.[3] There are many strange stories about the Servant Lamp that stood in the center of the Menorah. One such story has the "Lamp of God" mysteriously extinguished about the same time the Ark of the Covenant was captured by the Philistines. Do such stories have a prophetic significance for us today?

The History of the Menorah

In order to better understand the religious significance of the Menorah, let us review its history. We are told in the book of Exodus that Moses was instructed to build a golden lampstand upon which seven lamps were positioned:

The procession of Jewish slaves and their treasures shows a portrayal of the Temple Menorah in the Arch of Titus at Rome.

"And he made the candlestick of pure gold: of beaten work made he the candlestick; his shaft, and his branch, his bowls, his knobs, and his flowers, were of the same:

"And six branches going out of the sides thereof; three branches of the candlestick out of the one side thereof, and three branches of the candlestick out of the other side thereof:

The Arch of Titus stands in Rome, just south of the Forum. Through it runs the Appian Way, site of the processional of Jewish slaves after the destruction of Jerusalem in A.D. 70.

"Three bowls made after the fashion of almonds in one branch, a knob and a flower; and three bowls made like almonds in another branch, a knob and a flower: so throughout the six branches going out of the candlestick.

"And in the candlestick were four bowls made like almonds, his knobs, and his flowers:

The first Menorah was used in the Tabernacle built at Mount Sinai during the days of Moses.

"*And a knob under two branches of the same, and a knob under two branches of the same, and a knob under two branches of the same, according to the six branches going out of it.*

"*Their knobs and their branches were of the same: all of it was one beaten work of pure gold.*

"*And he made his seven lamps, and his snuffers, and his snuffdishes, of pure gold.*

"*Of a talent of pure gold he made it, and all the vessels thereof*" (Exodus 37:17-24).

The almond tree figured prominently in the design of the Menorah. The leaves, flowers, and fruit were featured, perhaps reminding us of Aaron's rod that budded. When the miracle occurred, his rod, having no root, bore leaves, flowers, and almonds overnight (Numbers 17:8). Furthermore, the Hebrew word for almond (*luz*) has become a root for "light" in other languages.

The first-century Jewish historian, Flavius Josephus, also described the Menorah built for Moses by Bezaleel:

> "Over against this table, near the southern wall, was set a **candlestick of cast gold**, hollow within, being of the weight of one hundred pounds, which the Hebrews call Chinchares; if it be turned into the Greek language, it denotes a talent. It was made with its knops, and lilies, and pomegranates, and bowls (which ornaments amounted to seventy in all); by which means the shaft elevated itself on high from a single base, and spread itself into as many branches **as there are planets, including the sun among them**. It terminated in seven heads, in one row, all standing parallel to one another; and these branches carried seven lamps, one by one, **in imitation of the number of planets**. These lamps looked to the east and to the south, the candlestick being situate obliquely."[4]

The Menorah was placed adjacent to the south wall, just across the room from the table of shewbread in the Holy Place of the Mosaic Tabernacle. It stood obliquely toward the east and toward the south. Some rabbinic sources say the three eastern lamps faced west—toward the center lamp and the three western lamps faced east—toward the center lamp. The fourth or center lamp faced northward toward the middle of the room.

This middle lamp was called *Ner Elohim*, the "Lamp of God" as well as *Shamash*, the "Servant Lamp." It was also called the "Western Lamp" because it stood just west of the three eastern lamps. Each lamp held "six eggs" measure of oil which would last one day.

The Miracle of the Menorah

Each morning, a priest would service the lamps, except the two most easterly. If he found any lamps extinguished, he relighted them. The two eastern lamps were left burning until after the morning service. The Servant Lamp was left burning all day and was refilled in the evening. There are stories that the *Shamash* would continue to burn for as much as a day longer on the same amount of oil. Rabbis called this "the miracle of the Menorah."

Solomon's Temple

When Solomon built his Temple, the Mosaic Menorah served in the new Holy Place. It was given a prominent position, though several lampstands were built and used throughout the complex.

What happened to that first Menorah remains a mystery. One accounts suggests an angel hid the Mosaic Menorah and other Temple artifacts in an underground chamber, beneath the Most Holy Place, just prior to the Babylonian destruction of the Temple in 587 B.C. When the third Temple is built, the angel should return, open the mysterious chamber, and retrieve the Temple furnishings.

Zerubbabel's Temple

After the Babylonian captivity, the exiles returned to Jerusalem and restored Temple worship. It is likely that one of Solomon's menorahs was used in the sanctuary built by Zerubbabel.

Antiochus Epiphanes

In 168 B.C., the Syrian general, Antiochus Epiphanes, sacked Jerusalem and stole the Menorah, along with the rest of the Temple treasury. Josephus wrote:

> "So he left the temple bare, and took away the **golden candlesticks**, and the golden altar of incense, and table of shewbread, and the altar of burnt offering; and did not abstain from even the veils, which were made of fine linen and scarlet. He also emptied it of its secret treasures, and left nothing at all remaining."[5]

He built an idol altar upon God's altar and slaughtered swine upon it. Josephus wrote that

the desecration was considered to be the predicted "abomination of desolation." It was thought
to be a fulfillment of Daniel's prophecy in Daniel
8:11-13. Three years later, on the 25th of Kislev,
165 B.C., Judas Maccabaeus drove the Syrians out
of Jerusalem and proceeded to cleanse the Temple.
They replaced the Menorah, altar, table, and other
furnishings with new items. Josephus reported:

> "When therefore he had carefully purged it, and had
> brought in **new** vessels, **the candlestick**, the table,
> and the altar, which were made of gold, he hung up the
> veils at the gates, and added doors to them. He also took
> down the altar of burnt offering, and built a new one of
> stones that he gathered together, and not of such as
> were hewn with iron tools. So **on the five and twen-
> tieth day of the month Kislev, they lighted the
> lamps that were on the candlestick**, and offered
> incense upon the altar, and laid the loaves upon the
> table, and offered burnt offerings upon the new altar."[6]

The Feast of Lights

They found only one day's oil supply for the
Menorah. It would take eight days to produce
another batch of oil. However, the priests serviced
the Lamps and lit them anyway. Those lamps
burned for eight days on one day's oil supply!

The miracle was looked upon as a special blessing from God. So the priesthood established the
festival of Dedication (*Hanukkah*) to commemorate the miracle. The festival is also called the

A typical Hanukkah menorah consists of nine candles. Eight of them represent the miraculous eight days the Temple Menorah burned with only one day's oil supply. The ninth candle (center) is the *Shamash* or Servant Candle.

Feast of Lights. Families celebrate the festival of Hanukkah with small menorahs at home featuring eight candles plus a servant candle for a total of nine. One candle is lit each day during the eight days of Hanukkah, using the fire of the Servant Candle.

Herod's Temple

The Menorah that stood in Herod's Temple may have been the one built by Judas Maccabaeus, because the Servant Lamp on that Menorah was said to burn longer than the other lamps. Upon the destruction of Herod's Temple in A.D. 70, the Romans carried the Menorah to Rome and paraded it through the streets. A stone relief of that parade, along with the Menorah, was carved into the Arch of Titus that stands along the Appian Way near the Forum in Rome to this day (see picture on page 14).

The Miracle of the Servant Lamp

A strange story is told about the Menorah and its Servant Lamp. According to the Jerusalem Talmud, Yoma 43:3, the "miracle of the Servant Lamp" ceased about 40 years before the Romans burned the Temple. The Servant Lamp simply refused to burn.

Simeon, the Righteous

The Jewish Encyclopedia says that the Lamp went out upon the death of "Simeon the Righteous, who was high priest in those days." And who was this Simeon? Was he the Simeon of Luke 2:25-36? The account tells of a certain Simeon, who was in the Temple when the one-month-old

Jesus was brought in by Joseph and Mary for His "Redemption of the Firstborn" ceremony.

According to certain details in the story, Simeon, the Righteous, and the Simeon in Luke's account could very well be one and the same.

*"... the same man was **just** and devout, waiting for the consolation of Israel: and the Holy Ghost was upon him.*

*"And it was revealed unto him by the Holy Ghost, that he should not **see death** before he had seen the Lord's Christ"* (Luke 2:26-26).

Note that his death was divinely delayed until he could see the promised Messiah. And in the Jerusalem Talmud account, when Simeon the Righteous died, the Servant Lamp went out. Both stories were centered around a death experience.

Luke's account does not refer to him as the high priest, but the story is set in the Temple. Furthermore, he had to be a priest in order to preside over the "Redemption of the Firstborn" ceremony. If he was not the high priest, and if he believed Jesus was the Messiah, he should have immediately fetched the high priest. Since the account does not say that he reported his find to the high priest, one may assume that he, himself, was the high priest.

Simeon took the child up in his arms and said, *"Lord, now lettest thou thy servant depart in peace, according to thy word"* (Luke 2:29). Again, the subject concerns Simeon's impending death. Simeon continued:

> *"For mine eyes have seen thy salvation, which thou hast prepared before the face of all people;* ***a light to lighten the Gentiles****, and the glory of thy people Israel"* (Luke 2:30-32).

He called Jesus a *"light to lighten the Gentiles!"* Indeed! It appears that Jesus was the fulfillment of this mysterious Servant Lamp in the Menorah!

The story in the Jerusalem Talmud places the time frame for the failure of the Servant Lamp at about 40 years before the destruction of the Temple. It seems odd that the lamp would fail during the ministry of Jesus.

Furthermore, as I understand the story, the problem continued for 40 years. Perhaps the crucifixion had something to do with it. The Talmud account says nothing about Jesus being the cause—only that "the miracle of the Menorah ceased upon the death of Simeon the Righteous, who was high priest in those days."

But the opening chapter of the book of Revelation gives a view of Jesus standing in the middle of a Menorah. John saw Him standing on the Servant Lamp and *"his countenance was like the sun shining in its strength"* (Revelation 1:16).

John, the writer of Revelation, attributes to Jesus the position of Servant Lamp. Somehow, this Servant Lamp must be connected to the events surrounding His crucifixion. More about this later.

The Mystery!

We realized that we had learned something here that could not be found in most theological commentaries. The concept begged for further investigation. That's when we began to see that almost all of the sevens in the Bible display a symbolic Servant Lamp in the fourth or middle position!

Once we came to realize the significance of the lampstand, we began to see dozens of menorahs throughout the Bible.

Chapter One Notes:

1. Edward Gibbon, *Decline and Fall of the Roman Empire*, Vol. 3, pp. 421-422.
2 . Ibid.
3. The Jewish Encyclopedia, *The Menorah* (Funk and Wagnalls Company, New York), Vol. VIII, p. 494.
4. Flavius Josephus, *Antiquities of the Jews*, Book III, Chapter VI, Paragraph 7.
5. *Antiquities of the Jews*, Book XII, Chapter V, Paragraph 4.
6. *Antiquities*, Book XII, Chapter VII, Paragraph 6.

Chapter Two

Menorahs of the Old Testament

Let's return to the opening chapters of the Bible and consider a startling series of menorahs.

Genesis 1:1 Forms a Menorah

The Bible opens with a menorah. Note the Hebrew text in Genesis 1:1:

בראשית ברא אלהים **את** השמים ואת הארץ:

ha'aretz · va'eht · hashamayim · **eht** · Elohim · barah · bereshit

These seven Hebrew words (reading from right to left) form the sentence: *Bereshit* [In the beginning] *barah* [created] *Elohim* [God] ***eht*** [aleph/tahv] *hashamayim* [the heavens] *vaeht* [and] *haeretz* [the earth].

The fourth word, את eht (pronounced as an eight), seems to represent a Servant Lamp. It contains two Hebrew letters—the א *aleph* and the ת *tahv*—the first and last letters of the *Aleph-beit*. They correspond to the Greek letters—Alpha and Omega, or the English letters—A and Z.

Rabbinic scholars call the א *aleph* and ת *tahv* "the word of creation." One rabbi wrote that in the beginning God created the א *aleph* and ת *tahv* with all the letters in between—and with that *Aleph-beit* then created all things.

The opening chapter of the book of Revelation has Jesus implying that he is the א *aleph* and the ת *tahv*. He is claiming the position of "the word of creation" featured in Genesis 1:1!

The First Seven Books
Of the Old Testament

The first seven books, Genesis through Judges, form a menorah. They correspond to seven thousand years of human history. The fourth book, Numbers, corresponds to the Servant Lamp. This book gives the account of Aaron lighting the Menorah:

> *"Speak unto Aaron, and say unto him, when thou lightest the lamps, the seven lamps shall give light over against the candlestick.*

> *"And Aaron did so; he lighted the lamps thereof over against the candlestick, as the LORD commanded Moses.*

"And this work of the candlestick was of beaten gold, unto the shaft thereof, unto the flowers thereof, was beaten work: according unto the pattern which the LORD had showed Moses, so he made the candlestick" (Numbers 8:2-4).

Seven Days of Creation

Ever wonder why God made the sun on the fourth day instead of the first day? It must be because the sun is the Servant Lamp of our universe. It provides light for the planets—Mercury, Venus, Earth (or Moon), Mars, Jupiter, and Saturn. These were the planets visible to early man.

With the sun positioned in the center of our solar system, God created the first menorah. Remember, Josephus reported that the design of the Menorah in the Mosaic Tabernacle represented the sun and the planets.

The Sun, center of our Solar System, like the center lamp of the Menorah, provides the light for the planets.

On the first day of creation God said, *"Let there be light."* But He created the sun on the fourth day in order to form a menorah framework for both the solar system and the seven days of creation.

Lucifer Rebels

At this point, we should consider the rebellion of Lucifer. He wanted to usurp the throne of God. For the purpose of this study, let us suggest that he wanted to be the Servant Lamp—as his name implies. Lucifer means "light bearer."

He was thrown out of heaven, however, and this fourth celestial body from the sun, namely the earth, became the battlefield upon which the war between good and evil would be fought.

For the purpose of our understanding the conflict between God and the devil, let us take note that the sun, created on Wednesday of creation week, was moved from the fourth position of our solar menorah to the first position—after which the first day of the week, Sunday, was named. The moon, after which Monday was named, appearing to be as large as the sun, was given the second position.

Mercury, who represents evil (with his eagles wings and serpent staff) was awarded the position of Servant Lamp, after which Wednesday was named.

From this arrangement, the days of our week are designated—Sunday for the sun, Monday for

Mercury was called Hermes by the Greeks and Odin among the teutonic tribes of northern Europe.

the moon, Tuesday for Mars, Wednesday for Mercury, Thursday for Jupiter, Friday for Venus, and Saturday for Saturn.

Since Mercury is the closest planet to the sun, may I suggest that it corresponds to the "covering cherub," Lucifer. Also, the tribe of Dan adopted the same symbols attributed to Mercury—the serpent and eagle. When the tabernacle was built at Mt. Sinai, Ahiezer, prince of the Danites changed the insignia of their tribe from a serpent to an eagle. Some 150 years before the birth of Christ, rabbis wrote that the prince of the tribe of Dan was Satan and suggested that Dan would produce the antichrist.[1]

Genesis 1:1-5

תורה

Hay, Vav, Resh, Tahv

בראשי֒ת֒ ברא אלהים אה השמים ואה הארץ: והארץ
היתה תהו ובהו וחשך על־פני תהום ורו֒ח אלהים מרחפת
על־פני המים: ויאמר אלהים יהי־אור ויהי־אור: וי֒רא אלהים
את־האור כי־טוב ויברל אלהים בין האור ובין החשך: ויקרא
אל֒הים לאור יום ולחשך קרא לילה ויהי־ערב ויהי־בקר יום

In the opening paragraph of Genesis, *Torah*, the Hebrew word for Law, is encoded at 50 letter intervals.

We can get a glimpse of this conflict between God and the devil at Calvary. When Jesus hung upon the cross, the sun went out for three hours. But Jesus defeated Satan that day and took His rightful place as *"the Bright and Morning Star"* (Revelation 22:16). Jesus holds the exalted position of Servant Lamp—as we can see in the opening chapter of Revelation.

The Five Books of Moses

Moses wrote the first five books of the Bible under the direct inspiration of God. He alone could not possibly have arranged so many menorahs as we have from Genesis through Deuteronomy. Only God could have designed these books and their multitude of sevens. In fact, from

Exodus 1:1-7 תורה
Hay, Vav, Resh, Tahv

ואלה שמות בני ישראל הבאים מצרימה את יעקב איש
וביתו באו: ראובן שמעון לוי ויהודה: יששכר זבולן ובנימן:
דן ונפתלי גד ואשר: ויהי כל-נפש יצאי ירך-יעקב שבעים
נפש ויוסף היה במצרים: וימת יוסף וכל-אחיו וכל הדור
ההוא: ובני ישראל פרו וישרצו וירבו ויעצמו במאד מאד

Also, in the opening paragraph of Exodus, *Torah*, the Hebrew word for Law, is encoded at 50 letter intervals.

a study of the sevens throughout the Bible, one can only conclude that the entire Bible must be of divine origin.

The Menorah of the Torah

Encoded in the first paragraph of Genesis, at 50 letter intervals, is תורה, the Hebrew word for *Torah*. If this were all we could find hidden in the first five books, we could relegate this find to coincidence. But תורה *Torah* is found encoded in the introductory paragraphs of Exodus, Numbers, and Deuteronomy as well!

In the first paragraphs of both Genesis and Exodus,תורה*Torah* is found at 50 letter intervals. The number 50 is significant because the Law

Numbers 1:1-4   הרות

Tahv, Vav, Resh, Hay

 וידבר יהוה אל-משה במדבר סיני באהל מועד באחד לחדש
השני בשנה השנית לצאתם מארץ מצרים לאמר: שאו את-
ראש כל-עדת בני-ישראל למשפחתם לבית אבתם במספר
שמות כל-זכר לגלגלתם: מבן עשרים שנה ומעלה כל-יצא
צבא בישראל תפקדו אתם לצבאתם אתה ואהרן: ואתכם

In the Opening paragraph of Numbers, *Torah*, the Hebrew word for Law, is encoded at 50 letter intervals—BACKWARDS!

was given on Mount Sinai on the 50th day after crossing the Red Sea.

Rabbis say that the number 50 is a transcendent number. Being one above 49 (which is 7x7), 50 represents deity, whereas 49 represents humanity.

In the books of Numbers and Deuteronomy, תורה, *Torah* is found encoded in the introductory paragraphs as הרות. *Torah* is spelled **BACKWARDS**! These backward spellings for *Torah* evidently represent opposite lamps to Genesis and Exodus in this five-lamp menorah. All four encoded תורה *Torahs* must be pointing to the Servant Lamp found in the first sentence of Leviticus! The personal name of יהוה *YAHWEH* is encoded at 8 letter intervals in the first sentence of Leviticus!

Deuteronomy 1:5-8

Tahv, Vav, Resh, Hay

מלך הבשן אשר-יושב בעשתרת באדרעי: בעבר הירדן
בארץ מוטב הואיל משה באר את‑הֿתורה הזאת לאמר:
יהוה אלהינו דבר אלינו בחרב לאמר רב-לכם שבת בהֿר
הזה: פנו וסעו לכם ובאו הר האמרי ואל-כל-שכניו בערבה
בהר ובשפלֿה ובנגב ובחוף הים ארץ הכנעני והלבנון עד-
הנהר הגדל נהר-פרת: ראה נֿתתי לפניכם את-הארץ באו

In verses 5-8 of Deuteronomy, *Torah,* **the Hebrew word for
Law, is encoded BACKWARDS at 49 letter intervals!**

Eight is also a transcendent number, being one
above seven. Seven represents perfect humanity
and eight represents deity.

Leviticus 1:1

Hay Vav Hay Yod

ויקרא אל-משֿה וידבר יהוֿה אליו מאֿהל מועד לאמר:

In the first verse of Leviticus, *Yahweh,* **the Hebrew word for
LORD is encoded at 8 letter intervals.**

The message is this: The תורה *Torah* (typified by 50)
comes from יהוה *YAHWEH* (typified by 8) and reflects
His glory. The encoding of the word, *Torah*, at 50 letter
intervals in Genesis, Exodus, and Numbers reflects
transcendent deity. And the encoding of YAHWEH at
8 letter intervals also reflects transcendent deity.

But in the book of Deuteronomy, the word for
תורה *Torah* is encoded backward (in verses 5-8) at
49 letter intervals! Why only 49? Why not 50?

The Word

To understand this strange descent from 50 to
49, we should take note that the name of the book,
Deuteronomy, is a Greek title for this fifth book of
Moses. Its Hebrew title is דברים *Devarim*—plural
for the WORD! Had the book of דברים *Devarim*
been translated literally into the Greek language,
the title would have been *"LOGOS."* But the 70
scholars who translated the Hebrew *Tenakh* into
Greek (300 years B.C.), decided to name the book
Deuteronomy, which means, "a copy," since the
Greek translation of God's WORD was only a copy
and not the original.

Could this fifth book of Moses have a connection
with Jesus? In the opening verses of the Gospel of
John, Jesus is introduced as the *Logos* (Word):

*"In the beginning was the **Word**, and the **Word**
was with God, and the **Word** was God.*

"The same was in the beginning with God.

*"All things were made by him; and without him was
not any thing made that was made"* (John 1:1-3).

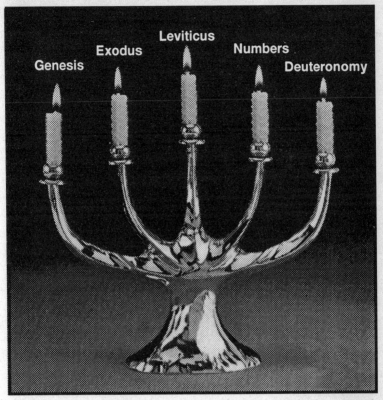

The five books of Moses are structured around the framework of a menorah—the four lamps of the Torah (Genesis, Exodus, Numbers, and Deuteronomy) reflect the glory of Yahweh, located in the center book (Leviticus).

The implication here is that the book of דברים (*Devarim* or Deuteronomy) represents Jesus, who condescended from His transcendent position of deity (typified by 50) to become a man (typified by 49). Therefore, the word תורה *Torah* appears to have been encoded at 49 letter intervals to show that the *"Word became flesh and dwelt among us."*

The First Seven Books

Genesis through Judges also form a menorah with the fourth book, Numbers, serving as the *Shamash* or Servant Lamp. It is remarkable that they also correspond to seven millennia of human history:

Genesis corresponds to the first millennium. Its subject is "death by sin." Even the very last verse of Genesis says, *"So Joseph died."*

Exodus corresponds to the second millennium. Its subject involves crossing a body of water. The story of the Red Sea follows the same general theme as the story of Noah's flood.

Leviticus corresponds to the third millennium. Its subject deals with praising God in the House of God. In like manner, the Tabernacle and Temple were built in the third millennium.

Numbers corresponds to the fourth millennium. Its subject concerns the 40-year exile of the Chosen People from their Promised Land. In like manner, the fourth millennium witnessed the Assyrian captivity in 722 B.C. and the Babylonian captivity in 606 B.C.

Deuteronomy corresponds to the fifth millennium. Its subject concerns the establishment of the government of God. In the opening chapter of Deuteronomy, Joshua (Yehoshua, whose name just happens to be practically the same as Jesus) is introduced and his message for Israel to take the kingdom was rejected. Moses then reminds the people, *"But Joshua the son of Nun, which standeth before thee, he shall go in thither: encourage him: for he shall cause Israel to inherit it"* (Deuteronomy 1:38). That incident appears to correspond to the fifth millennium and the rejection of Jesus' message that the *"kingdom of heaven is at hand."* It is that same Jesus, however, who will ultimately *"cause Israel to inherit it."*

Joshua, the sixth book of the Bible, corresponds to the sixth millennium. Its theme tells the story about the rejected Joshua becoming the accepted leader and fulfilling God's promise to Abraham that his seed will inherit the Promised Land. The last tribe is given the last parcel of land in Joshua 19:48! Does that correspond with 1948 or is it just a coincidence? The scenario appears to be a prophecy that the rejected Jesus will return to establish the long-awaited kingdom.

Judges, the seventh book, represents the seventh millennium. Its theme corresponds with the time when Christ will reign over the earth with a *"rod of iron"* during the great Sabbath rest.

The book of Judges is followed by Ruth, which tells the story of a Gentile bride. Until the third century, Ruth was attached as an appendix to Judges and, therefore, corresponds to events at the close of the seventh millennium. We can see that theme in Revelation 21 as the holy city, New Jerusalem, comes down from heaven *"prepared as a bride adorned for her husband."*

What we have in the five books of Moses and the succeeding books of Joshua, Judges, and Ruth are a comprehensive view of seven thousand years of human history—God's great plan of the ages. And they are structured as a series of menorahs layered upon menorahs.

God's plan for humanity covers a period of 7,000 years—itself forming the framework of another menorah, with the fourth millennium representing the Servant Lamp and its conflict between good and evil. The fourth millennium witnessed the Assyrian and Babylonian captivities. They seem to correspond with stories about the light of the Servant Lamp going out.

Seven Appearances to Abraham

There are seven divine appearances to Abraham which form the framework of a menorah, with the middle occasion corresponding to a Servant Lamp:

> *"And when the sun was going down, a deep sleep fell upon Abram; and, lo, a horror of great darkness fell upon him.*

> *"And it came to pass, that, when the sun went down, and it was dark, behold a smoking furnace and a burning lamp that passed between those pieces"* (Genesis 15:12,17).

The *"horror of a great darkness"* appears to be a prophecy of the suffering of Israel, and the lamp of God that appeared that night seems indicative of the Servant Lamp of the Menorah. It yielded hope and promise in the midst of darkness. I think it is a message to all of Abraham's descendants that there is a light of hope in the midst of difficulty—a blessed hope for a wonderful future. It will be realized when the Messiah, who is the Servant Lamp of God, appears to begin His reign in the seventh millennium.

Samuel and Eli

Another story of the Servant Lamp is found in I Samuel, chapter 3. It is the story of God's judgment upon a high priest, Eli, and his wicked sons, Hophni and Phinehas:

> *"And the child Samuel ministered unto to the LORD before Eli. And the word of the LORD was precious in those days; there was no open vision.*
>
> *"And it came to pass at that time, when Eli was laid down in his place, and his eyes began to wax dim, that he could not see;*
>
> *"And ere the **lamp of God** went out in the temple of the LORD, where the ark of God was, and Samuel was laid down to sleep"* (I Samuel 3:1-3).

According to the story, God came to Samuel with a message of judgment upon the house of Eli before the *"Lamp of God"* went out. Soon afterward, the Philistines captured the Ark of the Covenant and killed Hophni and Phinehas, the sons of Eli. When the news reached Eli, he fell over backward, broke his neck, and died. The wife of Phinehas gave birth to a son and died in childbirth. Upon her deathbed, she *"named the child Ichabod, saying, The glory is departed from Israel"* (I Samuel 4:21). The glory was gone; the ark was gone; and the family of the high priest was dead.

Evidently, the Servant Lamp on the Menorah in the Tabernacle went out that day. Could that Servant Lamp be part of a prophetic scenario? Could it correspond to the menorah that went out following the death of Simeon, the Righteous? Also, was the failure of the Servant Lamp really connected to Simeon's death or the death of another? Perhaps it was a prophecy fulfilled on the day of crucifixion.

Seven Last Sayings

That takes us to a scene outside the walls of Jerusalem where we witness yet another mysterious menorah. While hanging on the cross, Jesus made seven statements. Were they prophetic? Each of the seven sayings appears to represent a theme that corresponds with each of seven millennia of human history.

First, as He was nailed upon the cross at about 9:00

The seven last sayings of Christ correspond to a menorah and serve as a prophetic overview of human history.

in the morning, He said, *"Father, forgive them for they know not what they do"* (Luke 23:34). That prayer takes us all the way back to the first millennium and the guilty pair in the Garden of Eden.

His **second** saying, *"Today shalt thou be with me in paradise"* (Luke 23:43), reminds us of the second millennium, when God washed away the human race in the flood and gave Noah and his family a new opportunity to serve God.

His **third** saying, *"Woman, behold thy son!"* (John 19:26), reminds us of the third millennium when the LORD took Israel into His care. God brought Israel to Sinai and established the Mosaic covenant. Both the woman and the son were used as metaphors for Israel. From the burning bush God told Moses to tell Pharaoh, *"Israel is my son, my firstborn"* (Exodus 4:22). At Sinai, Israel became the wife of God.

According to the narrative of the crucifixion, at twelve noon the sun went out. The great Servant Lamp of our solar system refused to shine for three hours. Out of the darkness came the **fourth** saying of Jesus, *"My God, my God, why hast thou forsaken me?"* (Matthew 27:46).

This fourth saying represents the servant lamp gone out! The great battle with evil took Jesus all the way from the throne of God in heaven, to the place of God forsakenness!

Those three hours also seem to represent three thousand years of darkness for Israel, beginning with the splitting of the kingdom after the death of Solomon (about a thousand years B.C.) and will conclude with Jacob's trouble at the end of six thousand years.

At 3:00 p. m., the sun lighted up again. Christian theologians believe it was a prophecy that at the beginning of the seventh millennium, Jesus, who is the *Shamash*—the light of the world, will return.

His **fifth** saying, *"I thirst"* (John 19:28), reflects the cry of a lost soul. Since the beginning of the fifth millennium, the Gospel has provided the *"water of life"* to all who will believe.

His **sixth** saying, which I believe came just after the sun began to shine again, being the sixth hour, was, *"It is finished!"* (John 19:30).

It is the cry of triumph and is believed by Christians to be indicative of the Second Coming of Jesus at the close of the sixth millennium.

Finally, His **seventh** saying represents the conclusion of the seventh millennium, when he returns the kingdom to God, his father: *"Father, into thy hands I commend my spirit"* (Luke 23:46).

These seven sayings of Jesus form an awesome menorah that not only shows us that He had knowledge of all seven thousand years of human history, but that He, as the light of the world, the great Servant Lamp, was willing to suffer that much for us.

Old Testament Menorahs

As we have previously stated, Genesis through Judges/Ruth follow the framework of a seven-lamp

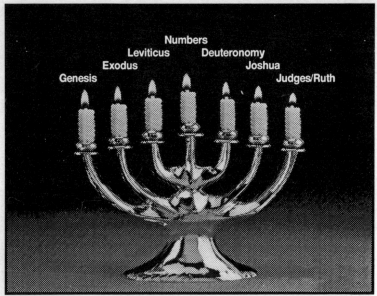

Genesis through Ruth appear to correspond to the framework of a menorah.

menorah. The realization of that great truth led us to consider the possibility that the rest of the Old Testament books follow the same framework. But there are 39 books of the Old Testament. How could we reconcile them with the concept of seven-lamp menorahs?

First, we learned that Flavius Josephus wrote that the Jews had collected 22 books which were considered to be divine. In his treatise "Against Apion," Josephus accused the Greek historians of lies and said that a true history was compiled in

"... twenty-two books which contain the records of all the past times; which are justly believed to be divine; and of them five belong to Moses, which contain his

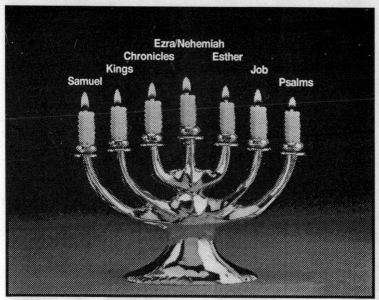

Samuel through Psalms appear to correspond to the framework of a second menorah.

laws and the traditions of the origin of the mankind till his death ... the prophets, who were after Moses, wrote down what was done in their times in thirteen books. The remaining four books contain hymns to God, and precepts for the conduct of human life."[2]

Furthermore, Origen (A.D. 185-254) listed the Old Testament books as 22; Ruth was attached to Judges; I & II Samuel were considered as one book, as were I & II Kings and I & II Chronicles; Ezra and Nehemiah were combined; Lamentations was a part of Jeremiah; and the twelve Minor Prophets were considered as one book. Thus, 39 books were reduced to 22. This view continued through at least the third century.

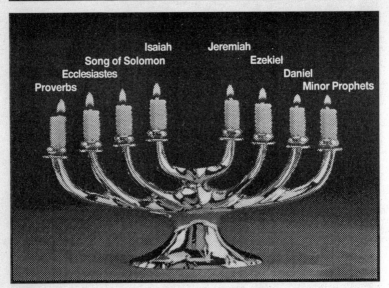

Proverbs through the Minor Prophets appear to correspond to the framework of a third menorah. The eight divisions can only mean that God has prepared for a Hanukkah menorah.

We noted that Ruth was once considered to be a part of the first seven books of the Old Testament as its theme rightly concludes the prophetic thrust of Judges. As we have already mentioned, Ruth, a Gentile bride, appears to correspond to the conclusion of the seventh millennium. It is at the end of the seventh millennium that the holy city, New Jerusalem, will descend out of heaven *"as a bride adorned for her husband."*

With the framework of the first menorah (Genesis-Judges/Ruth) settled, we began to consider the possibility that (1) Samuel, (2) Kings, (3) Chronicles, (4) Ezra/Nehemiah, (5) Esther, (6) Job, and (7) Psalms, would make up the framework of another menorah.

Ezra/Nehemiah would serve as the *Shamash* or Servant Lamp. Just as Leviticus, the *Shamash* of Genesis-Judges/Ruth carried the theme of building the Tabernacle and establishing a formal worship of God, Ezra/Nehemiah carries the theme of rebuilding the Temple and re-establishing a formal worship of God. It is practically the same theme.

The third menorah consists of the final set of books in the Old Testament: (1) Proverbs, (2) Ecclesiastes, (3) Song of Solomon, (4) Isaiah, (5) Jeremiah/Lamentations, (6) Ezekiel, (7) Daniel, and (8) the Twelve Minor Prophets. Here, however, we have a problem. There are eight divisions in this concluding menorah of Old Testament books. Why eight? The answer seems to lie in the story of Hanukkah.

The Prophecy of Hanukkah

In 520 B.C., two contemporary prophets, Haggai and Zechariah, added a new dimension to Jewish hopes of rebuilding their Temple and rekindling the spirit of Messianic fervor. Haggai (2:18-19) predicted a special blessing for the 24th day of Kislev. And Zechariah (4:1-7) predicted the addition of two more lamps on the Menorah.

First, Haggai was given the prophecy of Hanukkah:

"Consider now from this day and upward, from the four and twentieth day of the ninth month, even from the day that the foundation of the LORD'S temple was laid, consider it.

"... from this day will I bless you" (Haggai 2:18-19).

Haggai was told that a future blessing would come around that date.

Secondly, about the same time, autumn of 520 B.C., Zechariah was given a series of visions which correspond to Haggai's date. The implication that two more lamps would be added to Israel's Menorah can be seen in Zechariah's two olive trees:

"And the angel that talked with me came again, and waked me, as a man that is wakened out of his sleep,

*"And said unto me, What seest thou? And I said, I have looked, and behold a candlestick all of gold, with a bowl upon the top of it, and his **seven lamps** thereon, and seven pipes to the seven lamps, which are upon the top thereof:*

*"And **two olive trees** by it, one upon the right side of the bowl, and the other upon the left side thereof.*

*"Then he answered and spake unto me saying, This is the word of the LORD unto Zerubbabel, saying, **Not by might, nor by power, but by my spirit**, saith the LORD of hosts.*

"Who art thou, O great mountain? before Zerubbabel

thou shalt become a plain: and he shall bring forth the **headstone** *thereof with shoutings, crying,* **Grace, grace** *unto it"* (Zechariah 4:1-3,6-7).

In addition to the seven lamps of the Menorah, Zechariah was introduced to *"two olive trees,"* which in Revelation 11:4 are also called *"two candlesticks."* The implication is that these two lamps are added to the other seven, making a total of nine lamps—a Hanukkah menorah! And what do they represent?

First we are told that they correspond to a special work of the Holy Spirit: *"... not by might nor by power, but by my* **spirit** *..."* That was fulfilled on the day of Pentecost.

Second, they will bring forth the headstone (Messiah) and His covenant of Grace: *"... crying,* **Grace, grace** *..."* The fact that the term "grace" was repeated twice also seems to correspond to the additional two lamps and introduces the Dispensation of Grace with its new covenant, the New Testament!

In Revelation 11:4, we are told that two witnesses are fulfillments of the two olive trees in Zechariah's prophecy:

"These are the two olive trees, and the two candlesticks standing before the God of the earth" (Revelation 11:4).

Note that the two olive trees have now become two additional lamps on the menorah—making a

nine-lamp Hanukkah menorah! These two prophets, Haggai and Zechariah, direct our attention to
the events in 165 B.C.—the establishment of
Hanukkah by Judas Maccabeus.

So why do we have only eight divisions (see
picture on page 50) in this final menorah of Old
Testament books? Why not nine? Perhaps it is
because the Messiah had not yet arrived. These
Old Testament books had no Servant Lamp, only
eight divisions—corresponding to the eight days
in which the Temple Menorah burned using only
one day's oil supply.

The Messiah's coming was not a part of the Old
Testament. However, He was soon to come, and
bring with Him a new covenant (New Testament)
designed around the Hanukkah menorah! Just as
the Old Testament is designed after the menorah
of the Law, the New Testament, with its 27 books,
is designed after the fashion of three nine-lamp
Hanukkah menorahs, which we shall view in
Chapter Four. First, however, let us enlarge upon
this prophecy of Hanukkah by observing the Shield
of Israel—designed after Zechariah's vision.

Chapter Two Notes:

1. H. C. Kee, *"Testaments of the Twelve Patriarchs,"* in THE OLD
   TESTAMENT PSEUDEPIGRAPHA, Vol 1, ed. James H.
   Charlesworth (Garden City, NY: Doubleday, 1983), p. 809.
2. Flavius Josephus, *"Against Apion,"* Book I, Paragraph 8.

View from the top of the menorah. Note: three lamps on either side of center were turned to face the shamash or servant lamp.

View from beneath the lamps.

This menorah was built around the general design of the Lampstand taken by the Romans, a bas-relief of which can be seen in the Arch of Titus (pages 14 and 17). It features the leaves, flowers and fruit of the almond tree.

Chapter Three

The Shield
of Israel

"Then answered I, and said unto him, What are these two olive trees upon the right side of the candlestick and upon the left side thereof?" (Zech. 4:11).

Benjamin Netanyahu, a regular contributor to the JEWISH PRESS, is the head of Israel's conservative Likud party. One of his recent comments is of special interest. It appears in the July 16, 1993, issue of the PRESS as he writes on the subject of Israel's national history:

"The Menorah on the Arch of Titus was surely intended to represent the final destruction of Jewish sovereignty and the dissolution of the Jewish nation. Yet anyone in our own generation who has gazed up at it must feel that it represents the complete opposite. **For us the Menorah, which has been adopted as the shield for the State of Israel, represents the revival of the Jewish people and its return to its land."**

The Shield of Israel, also called "Coat of Arms," follows a design that corresponds with the vision seen by Zechariah—two olive branches standing beside Israel's Menorah.

The Menorah—the golden lampstand of the Tabernacle and both Temples—is perhaps the greatest of all Messianic symbols. Its seven arms represent the biblical number of completion. More than that, the arrangement of the Menorah elevates the *Shamash*, or Servant Lamp, to a position of dominance. This lamp occupies the fourth or center position among the other lights. It typifies the person and work of the Messiah.

While referring to the Roman conquest of Israel and the Arch of Titus, Mr. Netanyahu calls attention to a major point: the Menorah literally holds the hope of modern Israel. It reminds Jews of the Temple and the Levites' priestly service, but particularly of the Messiah, whom they believe will soon come to unite the land and its people in the Messianic Kingdom.

The Shield of Israel

It is quite interesting that the "shield of the State of Israel" to which Mr. Netanyahu refers appears on the official documents and currency of modern Israel. This shield is formed by the Temple Menorah, designed after the one on the Arch of Titus in Rome. It is flanked on each side by a stylized olive branch. Across the base of the shield, in Hebrew, is the word "Israel." The two olive branches are rooted in this word.

Its design reminds us of a biblical picture seen in the book of Zechariah. The Lord gives the prophet a special series of visions concerning both the first coming and future return of the Messiah. Chapter four relates an amazing vision of the golden Menorah, flanked by two olive trees. Somehow, the trees are connected to the Menorah by pipes which continually supply it with oil for the lamps. The sum of the imagery tells the story of Zerubbabel as the one commissioned to rebuild the Temple, following the Babylonian captivity.

In Hebrew, Zerubbabel means "born in Babylon." Following the captivity, he was appointed governor in Jerusalem and became its most active political leader. Among his contemporaries were Haggai and Zechariah, who were used by God to urge him to complete the work of Temple rebuilding.

In particular, Zechariah's prophecy holds the promise that Zerubbabel will, by the power of God's Spirit, succeed in the work of restoring the Temple. This promise is sealed with the vision of the Menorah and two olive branches.

As Christians, it is easy for us to see that the Menorah symbolizes Jesus, *"the light of the world"* (John 9:5). And just as clearly, the oil for the lamps is the obvious symbol of the Holy Spirit. As the prophet inquires about the vision, he is specifically told, *"Not by might, nor by power, but by my **spirit**, saith the Lord of Hosts"* (Zechariah 4:6).

Still, Zechariah was puzzled by the picture. The angel had told him that Zerubbabel was ordained to finish the Temple, but he wanted to know more about the outworking of God's power. He asked the angel for a further explanation. The dialogue went as follows:

> "*Then answered I, and said unto him, What are these two olive trees upon the right side of the candlestick and upon the left side thereof?*
>
> "*And I answered again, and said unto him, What be these two olive branches which through the two golden pipes empty the golden oil out of themselves?*
>
> "*And he answered me and said, Knowest thou not what these be? And I said, No, my lord.*
>
> "*Then said he, These are the two anointed ones, that stand by the Lord of the whole earth*" (Zech. 4:11-14).

The Two Witnesses

Thus, the image of two olive branches flanking the golden Menorah becomes the symbol of the power behind the rebuilding of the Temple. It is the shield of modern Israel. In Zechariah's day, the second Temple was the object of God's power. However, there will be a future day when still another Temple will be built. Jews the world over long for the building of the third Temple. Most of them believe that Messiah, Himself, will be its designer and builder. But actually, in the design of their shield, they acknowledge "... *the two anointed ones ...*" who will bring God's plan for the rebuilding of the Temple into action.

In the book of Revelation, these two individuals appear again, in a setting that is remarkably similar to the one presented to Zechariah. Significantly, it is also connected with the rebuilding of a Temple:

> *"And there was given me a reed like unto a rod: and the angel stood, saying, Rise and measure the temple of God, and the altar, and them that worship therein.*
>
> *"But the court which is without the temple leave out, and measure it not; for it is given unto the Gentiles: and the holy city shall they tread under foot forty and two months.*
>
> *"And I will give power unto my two witnesses, and they shall prophesy a thousand two hundred and three-score days, clothed in sackcloth.*
>
> *"These are the two olive trees and the two candlesticks standing before the God of the earth"* (Rev. 11:1-4).

It is widely believed that these two witnesses represent the Holy Spirit's two branches of action, as seen in the Old Testament. They are the Law and the Prophets. Moses and Elijah are usually suggested as the highest fulfillment of these two exalted offices. In the Revelation passage, it is obvious that the two are positioned just as they were in the days of Zerubbabel. They are present to provide the impetus for Temple building. Their role is that of exhortation and empowerment. After the return from Babylon, the land was uncultivated and teeming with enemies. The leaders needed their spiritual foundation to move forward.

In the future, the power of the two witnesses will stand in opposition to the force of the antichrist, who will claim the right to the throne and the Temple. Revelation shows them standing in opposition to the beast, or the system of the antichrist. They give their lives, then stand in resurrection before the enemies who thought they had been destroyed for good. They stand bodily as a shield of protection against Israel's enemies, exactly fulfilling the type and symbol of Israel's shield, with its olive branches and seven-branched Menorah.

The Menorah of Hanukkah

But there is another menorah—the lamps of Hanukkah. Its nine branches commemorate an event that occurred in 165 B.C., as a famous man became a type of the antichrist. His name was Antiochus IV Epiphanes. He was determined to destroy the Jewish religion by forbidding them to practice the rituals of the Law of Moses. He issued decrees against observance of the Sabbath, feast days, circumcision and other important Jewish rites. He even destroyed copies of the Torah.

In the Temple, he set up an idolatrous altar, featuring the worship of the Olympian Zeus. The altar to Zeus was erected on the traditional altar of burnt offering. There, he offered the flesh of a swine. Furthermore, he ordered that on the 25th of every month thereafter, this offering be repeated in anniversary of his own birthday.

But in the end, he underestimated the dedication and response of Judaism's righteous remnant. His actions sparked the Maccabean revolt, in which his armies were finally defeated by heroic Jewish forces. On the 24th of Kislev of 165 B.C.—three years to the day after its desecration—the Temple was cleansed and dedicated.

The central feature of this dedication has come to be memorialized in the Jewish feast of Hanukkah. Its symbol is the nine-branched menorah, with its Servant Lamp and eight branches, each of which stands for one day of the eight-day festival. The story is told that when the Temple was cleansed and rededicated, only one day's supply of consecrated oil could be found for the Menorah. But miraculously, this supply lasted for eight days, until new oil could be consecrated. Eight is the biblical number of the new birth—of fullness or abundance.

What is amazing about this is that the two olive branches in Zechariah's vision empty themselves into the menorah by way of "... *two golden pipes ...*" which, in themselves, may be viewed as two additional arms on the menorah—making nine.

The Promise of a New Covenant—Grace

*"Who art thou, O great mountain? before Zerubbabel thou shalt become a plain: and he shall bring forth the **headstone** thereof with shoutings, crying, **Grace, grace** unto it"* (Zech. 4:7).

This nine-branched menorah is not associated with the law, but with grace. The promise of the *"headstone"* points to Jesus Christ—the stone which the builders rejected (Acts 4:11). Through His rejection and sacrifice at Calvary, a new covenant was instituted—the covenant of *"Grace."* The coming of the Holy Spirit on the day of Pentecost (Acts 2) was a Divine act of dedication for this new dispensation of Grace. The Holy Spirit was poured out upon a new temple structure—the body of believers. Thus a new temple was dedicated on Pentecost—Hanukkah fulfilled.

The original Menorah, given to Moses during the Exodus, spoke of the illumination that was to come through God's Anointed One. The Hanukkah Menorah stands for all that, while additionally featuring the number eight (a new beginning) plus one (the Servant Candle). Taken as a whole, they speak of the number nine, associated with the nine blessings of the Beatitudes (Matt. 5:3-11) and the ninefold *"... fruit of the Spirit"* (Gal. 5:22).

Therefore, when we look closely at the modern shield of Israel, we notice that the two olive branches are spaced closely against the left and right branches of the Temple Menorah. Furthermore, the tip of each branch looks like a flame, giving the impression of the nine-branched menorah of Temple dedication! At last, we see what the vision of Zechariah means. The shield of Israel is a nine-branched Hanukkah menorah!

The seven-branched Menorah was designed after the Almond tree with its leaves, flower and fruit. But the two additional branches which make up the Hanukkah menorah are from the Olive tree. It is interesting to note that the apostle Paul addressed the subject of the olive tree in Romans 11:17-24. In verses 17-18, Paul refers to Gentile believers as a wild olive tree:

> *"And if some of the branches be broken off, and thou, being a **wild olive tree**, wert grafted in among them, and with them partakest of the root and fatness of the olive tree;*
> *"Boast not against the branches. But if thou boast, thou bearest not the root, but the root thee"* (Romans 11:17-18).

Gentile Christianity is indeed guilty of boasting against the good olive tree—Israel. Historically, early Roman Christian theologians believed that God had forever forsaken Israel and that the New Testament Church had fallen heir to all that God promised to Israel. They could not have been more wrong! Paul makes it clear that after many years of exile from their land, God will graft the Jews back into the good Olive tree—Israel:

> *"For if thou wert cut out of the olive tree which is wild by nature, and wert grafted contrary to nature into a good olive tree: how much more shall these, which be the natural branches, be grafted into their own olive tree?"* (v. 24).

The "breaking off" and "grafting back in" is a fact of history. The nation was broken in A.D. 70 with the burning of the Temple and A.D. 135 with the long exile from their land. The grafting back began in this century—with the highlight year being 1948. The grafting in continues until the Messiah arrives to set up His long-awaited kingdom.

Each olive branch on the shield of Israel is designed with 12 leaves and 12 olives. They represent the twelve tribes of Israel. Atop each branch shines the flame of the Holy Spirit. Added to the seven lamps, they make a Hanukkah menorah. Note, however, that there are a total of 24 leaves and 24 olives. But there are not 24 tribes of Israel, only 12. Is it possible then, that one of those branches could represent a wild olive branch having been grafted in? How else could history explain the phenomenon of a Gentile Christianity displaying faith in a Jewish Christ for these past 2,000 years?

For Israel, the Holy Temple is the center of life. Among the Jews, it is said that any generation which does not attempt to rebuild the Temple is like the generation that allowed it to be torn down. With zeal, Jews look forward to the building of the third Temple. In their view, it will bring the Messianic era that will usher in the Kingdom age and the revived spirit of Israel. Zechariah's vision looks into that future age and offers the promise that the Temple will indeed be rebuilt, with the help of God's two witnesses.

A Shield of Hope

Amazingly, the modern shield of Israel looks both backward and forward, as it recalls the building of the second Temple and foreshadows the building of the third Temple.

Modern Jews revere the law of Moses and the person of Elijah, who is prophesied to come before the Tribulation. This hope is expressed in the closing verses of the Old Testament:

> *"Remember ye the law of Moses my servant, which I commanded unto him in Horeb for all Israel, with the statutes and judgments.*
> *"Behold, I will send you Elijah the prophet before the coming of the great and dreadful day of the Lord:*
> *"And he shall turn the heart of the fathers to the children, and the heart of the children to the fathers, lest I come and smite the earth with a curse"* (Malachi 4:4-6).

Benjamin Netanyahu is right when he says that the shield of Israel "represents the revival of the Jewish people and its return to its land." Its two olive branches represent several prophecies—among them is the promise of two very real people who will one day play a key role in restoring the spiritual life of the Jewish people and their Holy Temple.

Chapter Four

Hanukkah Menorahs of the New Testament

There are twenty-seven books in the New Testament corresponding to three Hanukkah menorahs of nine lamps each! The New Testament fulfills the prophecy of Hanukkah which Haggai 2:18-19 predicted:

> *"Consider now from this day and upward, from the four and twentieth day of the ninth month ... consider it ... from this day will I bless you."*

In 165 B.C., Judas Maccabaeus launched a new era in Jewish history. The observance of Hanukkah is historically linked to the birth of Jesus and a new dispensation of God's grace to mankind.

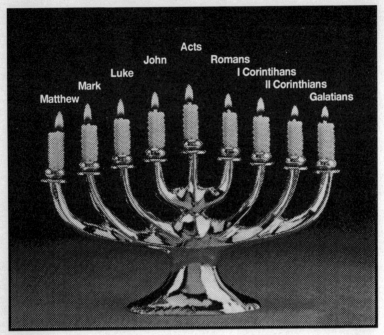

Matthew through Galatians appears to correspond to a nine-lamp Hanukkah menorah.

Matthew through Galatians

The first set of nine books, Matthew through Galatians, offers the first of three successive Hanukkah menorahs.

The Acts of the Apostles, being the 5th book and the Servant Lamp of this first Hanukkah menorah, features the Holy Spirit. He opened a new dispensation of grace on the day of Pentecost:

> *"And there appeared unto them cloven tongues like as of fire, and it sat upon each of them"* (Acts 2:3).

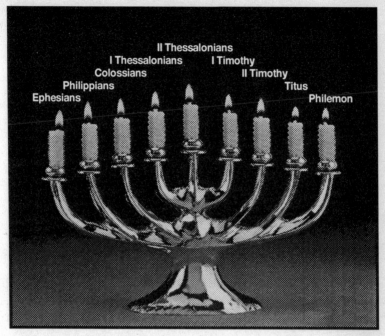

Ephesians through Philemon appears to correspond to the framework on a second nine-lamp Hanukkah menorah.

Ephesians through Philemon

The following set of nine books, Ephesians through Philemon, offers the second Hanukkah menorah, in which II Thessalonians, being the 5th book and Servant Lamp, features Jesus Christ:

> "And then shall that Wicked be revealed, whom the Lord shall consume with the spirit of his mouth and shall destroy with the brightness of his coming"
> (II Thessalonians 2:8).

Christ is viewed as a light or lamp—the *"brightness of His coming"*—who returns at the end of this age.

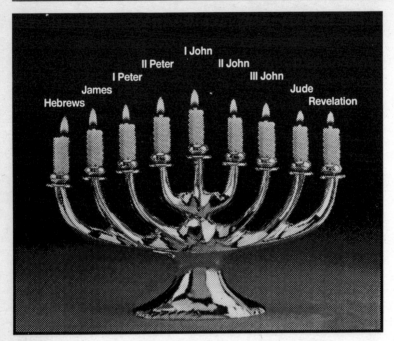

Hebrews through Revelation appears to correspond to the framework of a third nine-lamp Hanukkah menorah.

Hebrews through Revelation

The third set of nine books, Hebrews through Revelation, offers the third Hanukkah menorah. The fifth book and Servant Lamp, is the small epistle of I John. It features God, the Father:

"This then is the message which we have heard of him, and declare unto you, that God is light, and in him is no darkness at all" (I John 1:5).

These three are also discussed in the Old Testament. The Holy Spirit corresponds to the Old Testament Shekinnah Glory; Jesus corresponds to the promised Messiah; and God is viewed as the Creator of us all.

The nine books, Hebrews through Revelation, appear to be juxtapositioned to show the chronology of the end-time. Hebrews, the 19th book of the New Testament, appears to be a message prophetically designed for today's modern Jew; James through Jude appear to follow the chronology of the seven-year Tribulation Period; while Revelation concludes with the details leading to the arrival of Messiah.

James Through Jude

The letters of the Apostles to the early church have stood as beacons throughout the Church Age. Their sound doctrine has defined church structure and behavior. They have provided guidance and edification for millions of believers, past and present. They also contain a great many prophecies that directly apply to the latter days.

Some of those prophecies seem to lie in the relative arrangement or juxtaposition of biblical passages. Their placement, relative to other books of the Bible, actually seems to create a pattern that carries a prophetic message.

More specifically, the seven epistles that are positioned between Hebrews and Revelation appear to foreshadow the Great Tribulation!

At first glance, it seems unlikely that such a thing could be possible. But the more we look, the more obvious the picture becomes. As we look at these seven epistles in order, we will interpret their overall message by taking note of the general sense of each one. We want to emphasize that as originally delivered, these epistles were intended for the Church. But what of that future time when the Church, as such, has been removed from the world? Year by year, the seven letters take us through the Tribulation, setting the tone and outlining the general events of that time.

Year One of the Tribulation Period as Described by the Epistle of James

We'll begin by observing that in the confusing and tumultuous days following the catching away of the Church, many will try to understand what's happening. No doubt, they will begin to scrutinize the pages of the Bible. It is a certainty, for example, that members of national Israel's righteous remnant, finding themselves at the center of the conflict, will be led by the Holy Spirit to seek answers in the Word of God—including especially the New Testament, which they will discover to be divinely-inspired Scripture. In the seventh chapter of Revelation, these 144,000 Israelites are shown being sealed for God's service during the *"time of Jacob's trouble."*

Imagine their excitement when, on one future day, they open the book of James and come upon these words:

> *"James, a servant of God and of the Lord Jesus Christ, to the twelve tribes which are scattered abroad, greeting.*
> *"My brethren, count it all joy when ye fall into divers temptations.*
> *"Knowing this, that the trying of your faith worketh patience"* (James 1:1-3).

Surely, they will be amazed to discover that the letter from James is addressed to them! And along with the greeting, they will be gratified to observe that the letter contains words of comfort, written to a people experiencing Tribulation.

Of course, the Tribulation Period begins when the Lord opens a sealed book and judgment falls upon the earth. As the seals are broken, four horsemen are released and begin their plundering horrendous ride. War, economic depression, famine, and pestilence rage across the earth. The language of James describes this precise condition:

> *"If a brother or sister be naked, and destitute of daily food,*
> *"And one of you say unto them, Depart in peace, be ye warmed and filled: notwithstanding ye give them not those things which are needful to the body; what doth it profit?*
> *"Even so faith, if it hath not works is dead, being alone"* (James 2:15-17).

Certainly, this statement is one of general principle, valid throughout the Church Age. But more than that, it sets the scene of the physical and financial chaos that will reign in the Tribulation.

James 5 is one of the most important prophecies in the Bible. It opens with an proclamation of doom for certain *"rich men,"* who have *"heaped together treasure for the last days."* These men, the text explains, while living in pleasure, have unfairly deprived the faithful worker of his rightful wages:

> *"Be patient, therefore, brethren, unto the coming of the Lord. Behold the husbandman waiteth for the precious fruit of the earth and hath long patience for it until he receive the early and latter rain.*
>
> *"Be ye also patient; stablish your hearts: for the coming of the Lord draweth nigh.*
>
> *"Grudge not one against another, brethren, lest ye be condemned: behold, the judge standeth before the door"* (James 5:7-9).

Clearly, the language of this passage speaks of the events just prior to the coming of the Righteous Judge at the end of the Tribulation. Once again, it picks up the theme of the seal judgments, and the catastrophic economic failure that comes with the downfall of a global system of commerce. Certain rich men believe they can control the world by controlling its economy—they are wrong.

James concludes with a reference to one famous Old Testament prophet. We shouldn't be surprised to find that it is Elijah, of whom we read in Malachi 4:5:

> *"Behold, I will send you Elijah the prophet before the coming of the great and dreadful day of the Lord."*

And in James 5:17, we discover that his coming is beautifully foreshadowed:

> *"Elias* [Elijah] *was a man subject to like passions as we are, and he prayed earnestly that it might not rain: and it rained not on the earth by the space of three years and six months."*

Not only is Elijah mentioned here, but the time of his witness during the first half of the Tribulation is also foreshadowed. For three and one-half years, he will appear on earth as one of the two witnesses. Revelation 11:6 says, *"These have power to shut heaven, that it rain not in the days of their prophecy."* This is exactly the period mentioned both by James and Revelation 11:3. The coming of Elijah is an event longed for by every Jew since the diaspora. They look for him as a herald of the Messiah.

It seems then, that the epistle of James foreshadows the events that will open the Tribulation. When read by those who possess spiritual understanding, his epistle will give great hope to a people struggling through the first miserable months of God's wrath.

Year Two of the Tribulation Period as Described by the First Epistle of Peter

This epistle—the second in the series of seven epistles—is addressed to *"the strangers scattered"* throughout Asia Minor. In Peter's day, these would have been the early Hebrew Christians, struggling to remain faithful to God under the hostile Roman Empire. For the purposes of our prophetic overview, this sets the tone for the second year of the Tribulation. It should come as no surprise that the theme of this book is *"suffering"* for the cause of Christ.

Chapter 1, verses 5-7 describes the position of those who are suffering:

> *"Who are kept by the power of God through faith unto salvation ready to be revealed in the last time.*
> *"Wherein ye greatly rejoice, though now for a season, if need be, ye are in heaviness through manifold temptations:*
> *"That the trial of your faith, being much more precious than of gold that perisheth, though it be tried with fire, might be found unto praise and honour and glory at the appearing of Jesus Christ"* (I Peter 1:5-7).

The salvation mentioned here could be interpreted as the glorious appearing of the Lord at the end of the Tribulation. Note that the recipients of the letter are said to be suffering *"for a season."* This reminds us of the limited time of the Tribulation. As Jesus said:

"And except those days should be shortened, there should no flesh be saved: but for the elect's sake those days shall be shortened" (Matthew 24:22).

In chapter 2, verse 11, they are called *"strangers and pilgrims,"* and in the following verse, they are urged to be *"honest among the Gentiles."* This tells us that the audience here is Jewish. As in the book of James, we find that the letter is addressed to Hebrew Christians. Just as it was in the first century, the mandate here is not to overthrow existing Gentile governments, but to further the cause of Christ under the existing Roman rule. So it will be in the days of the future revived Roman Empire.

As we have noted, Peter writes this letter to Hebrew Christians under Roman jurisdiction in Asia Minor. He concludes the letter by sending greetings from *"the church that is at Babylon,"* and *"Marcus my son."* The introductory notes by the editors of the OPEN BIBLE suggest:

> "This epistle was written from Babylon (5:13), but scholars are divided as to whether this refers literally to Babylon in Mesopotamia or symbolically to Rome. There is no tradition that Peter went to Babylon, and in his day it had few inhabitants. On the other hand, tradition consistently indicates that Peter spent the last years of his life in Rome."

They observe that Mark was known to be in Rome during Paul's first imprisonment, and that his presence with Peter would be normal under

those circumstances. If this is true, it means that
Peter viewed the Roman Empire as Mystery
Babylon the Great! This, of course, is the system
that gives birth to the antichrist during the Tribulation, and a major theme in the book of Revelation.

As we have mentioned, the central theme of this
letter is personal conduct in suffering. The intent
of Peter's letter is to show that much of this
suffering will come in the form of unjust personal
attacks. Peter makes this plain:

> "And who is he that will harm you, if ye be followers
> of that which is good?
> "But and if ye suffer for righteousness' sake, happy are
> ye: And be not afraid of their terror, neither be troubled"
> (I Peter 3:13-14).

A few verses after this exhortation is given
(verses 19-20), Peter includes the example of
Christ's suffering for the sins of a dying humanity.
He also incorporates the story of the Lord's proclamation of victory to the spirits imprisoned in
the underworld. His illustration features Noah:

> "By which also he went and preached unto the spirits
> in prison;
> "Which sometime were disobedient, when once the
> longsuffering of God waited in the days of Noah, while
> the ark was a preparing, wherein few, that is, eight
> souls were saved by water" (I Peter 3:19-20).

The inclusion of this story reminds us of Jesus'
own words about the Tribulation Period, in which

He said, *"But as the days of Noe were, so shall also the coming of the Son of man be"* (Matt. 24:37). Jesus uses the figure of the great flood to explain that the Tribulation judgment will come in an unheralded way, just like the waters that destroyed a sinful world. That this picture is included in First Peter emphasizes the fact that the *"time of Jacob's trouble"* is foreshadowed here.

In I Peter 4:12-13, we read:

> *"Beloved, think it not strange concerning the fiery trial which is to try you, as though some strange thing happened unto you:*
> *"But rejoice, inasmuch as ye are partakers of Christ's sufferings; that, when his glory shall be revealed, ye may be glad also with exceeding joy"* (I Peter 4:12-13).

Here, we find words of exhortation that mention the revealing of Christ in His glory at the Second Coming. This is an exact statement of the situation that will exist for the saints in the Tribulation. This thought is echoed in chapter 5, verse 4:

> *"And when the chief Shepherd shall appear, ye shall receive a crown of glory that fadeth not away"* (I Peter 5:4).

For the saints of the Tribulation, suffering with grace will become much easier, as they cling to the hope that Christ will soon appear in glory to judge His enemies.

Year Three of the Tribulation Period as Described by the Second Epistle of Peter

This epistle is addressed *"to them that have obtained like precious faith with us ..."* No longer is the message specifically directed toward the righteous remnant of Israel. From the prophetic viewpoint, this letter is aimed at the Tribulation saints.

In this epistle, there is an urgency, followed by a warning against the threat of an imminent danger. It begins in the tenth verse of chapter one:

> *"Wherefore the rather, brethren, give diligence to make your calling and election sure: for if ye do these things, ye shall never fall"* (II Peter 1:10).

What things? The first nine verses paint a picture of Christian virtue, which the believer is urged to incorporate into his own life. Only through the spiritual growth that comes through godly living will the believer be kept from falling in these days of judgment.

In verses 14-15, Peter refers to his body as a *"tabernacle."* This is the witness of God, which, along with the Word of God that comes to believers through the Scriptures, provides protection from Satan's deceptions. It is interesting that such false teachings and their proponents are the subject of the rest of this epistle.

It is also interesting that the midpoint of the

Tribulation is couched in exactly the same terms. The beast of Revelation rises up against God and His witnesses:

> *"And he opened his mouth in blasphemy against God, to blaspheme his name, and his tabernacle, and them that dwell in heaven"* (Revelation 13:6).

Peter writes about latter-day false teachers, who introduce *"damnable heresies"* into the community of the believing remnant. But he quickly adds a note of hope, saying that just as God judged the fallen angels and sinful man during the flood, so He will judge those who mislead the people. In this second of his two epistles, Peter again makes reference to the great flood, which becomes a figure of the judgment of humanity during the Great Tribulation.

The third chapter of the letter is a latter-day prophecy, the subject of which is to be found in verse 10: *"the day of the Lord."* In other words, the Tribulation is in view here. He reminds his readers that this horrific period of time will not only come, but that it is God's judgment. In verses 11-12, he urges his readers to Godly living:

> *"Seeing then that all these things shall be dissolved, what manner of persons ought ye to be in all holy conversation and godliness,*
> *"Looking for and hasting unto the coming of the day of God, wherein the heavens being on fire shall be dissolved, and the elements shall melt with fervent heat?"* (II Peter 3:11-12).

He reminds the Tribulation saints that though they are going through the worst judgment ever to befall mankind, they must remember that ultimately, creation will be cleansed.

Year Four of the Tribulation Period as Described by the First Epistle of John

The letter is generally directed toward the *"breth-ren"* (1:7), and *"little children"* (2:18). It is in the latter verse that the central message is to be found:

> *"Little children, it is the last time: and as ye have heard that **antichrist shall come**, even now are there many antichrists; whereby we know that it is the last time"* (I John 2:18).

Who should appear at this point but the antichrist! Certainly, this message has long applied to the Church Age. But it will apply with even greater accuracy during the dark days of the Tribulation Period. An important thought here is that the word "antichrist" is to be found three times in this epistle and once in the one that follows it. Nowhere else in the New Testament is this word to be found!

The introduction of the antichrist is juxtapositioned in I John precisely because it is the fourth and middle book among these seven epistles between Hebrews and Revelation. It points up the teaching that the antichrist will make his clandestine *"abomination of desolation"* around the middle of the Tribulation Period—at the three and one-half year point—halfway through the fourth year!

Note that John uses the phrase, *"it is the last time,"* in the present tense. In one sense, the Church Age may be defined as the last time. But during the Tribulation, this statement will be true in the most literal sense. John's declaration will one day speak with special clarity. Jesus' own statement about the Tribulation in Matthew carries the same message:

> *"Then if any man shall say unto you, Lo, here is Christ, or there; believe it not.*
> *"For there shall arise false Christs, and false prophets, and shall shew great signs and wonders; insomuch that, if it were possible, they shall deceive the very elect"* (Matthew 24:23-24).

The focus of John's first epistle is the walk of love; walking in the light, in fellowship with the Father, in spite of the darkness that prevails. Believers are urged to love one another in spiritual purity while doing the work of Christ. But all this is set in the context of an overwhelming evil:

> *"Who is a liar but he that denieth that Jesus is the Christ? He is **antichrist**, that denieth the Father and the Son"* (I John 2:22).

And again in the fourth chapter, verse 3, John

emphasizes the contrast between the believer dwelling in the light, and the conditions that prevail in the world:

> *"And every spirit that confesseth not that Jesus Christ is come in the flesh is not of God: and this is that spirit of **antichrist**, whereof ye have heard that it should come; and even now already is it in the world"* (I John 4:3).

As detailed by John in this epistle, the walk of love is no mere exercise of theory. It is a vital necessity, given the fierceness of the day. Read in the context of the Tribulation, I John 4:16-17 take on an entirely new meaning:

> *"And we have known and believed the love that God hath to us. God is love; and he that dwelleth in love dwelleth in God, and God in him.*
> *"Herein is our love made perfect, that we may have boldness in the day of judgment: because as he is, so are we in this world"* (I John 4:16-17).

In chapter 5, believers are urged to be overcomers, and to have assurance in the saving grace of the Lord. He urges them to be strong and to know that they can have confidence, in spite of the prevailing conditions.

The last sentence of the letter adds a warning note that will become especially profound during the Tribulation:

> *"Little children, keep yourselves from idols. Amen"* (I John 5:21).

This sentence reminds us of the ultimate idol, as the antichrist sits in the Temple and demands that he be worshiped as God. In Revelation 13:15, the word *"image"* might just as well be translated "idol."

"And he had power to give life unto the image of the beast, that the image of the beast should both speak, and cause that as many as would not worship the image of the beast should be killed" (Revelation 13:15).

Year Five of the Tribulation Period as Described by the Second Epistle of John

This brief epistle of only 13 verses is addressed to *"the elect lady and her children."* Many have speculated about her identity, some saying that perhaps she was the living mother of a family at the time John wrote the letter. This may, in fact, be true. But there are no historical documents to support it. Metaphorically, most expositors say that she represents the bride of Christ.

But suppose for a moment that she represents the elect of Israel. If this is the case, she depicts the 144,000 from among the 12 tribes. She is bearing the main burden of spreading the Gospel during the *"time of Jacob's trouble."*

She is urged to walk in truth and love, in spite of certain false teachers who dominate the spiritual landscape. Verse 7 makes this clear:

*"For many deceivers are entered into the world, who confess not that Jesus Christ is come in the flesh. This is a deceiver and an **antichrist**"* (II John 7).

Here, we find the Bible's final mention of this evil man by name. As he bedevils the Tribulation Saints, he weaves a supreme deception. John declares that only those who hold to the sound doctrine of the Apostles will survive spiritually.

The picture here may be clarified by remembering that Revelation 12:1 features the amazing depiction of an *"elect lady."*

"And there appeared a great wonder in heaven; a woman clothed with the sun, and the moon under her feet, and upon her head a crown of twelve stars" (Revelation 12:1).

This woman is Israel. She is shown giving birth to the Messiah. And now, during the great Tribulation, she must flee into the wilderness for 1,260 days—the last three and one-half years of the Tribulation Period. She is at the center of a battle in the heavens in which the angels of Israel's protector, Michael, and the dragon called Satan, fight a bitter battle over God's *"elect lady."* No doubt, the antichrist is in the vanguard of those who would see Israel annihilated.

The epistle ends on a very curious note that seems to bear directly on the theme of the Tribulation:

"Having many things to write unto you I would not write with paper and ink: but I trust to come unto you, and speak face to face, that our joy may be full.

"The children of thy elect sister greet thee. Amen" (II John 12-13).

Here the Apostle expresses a desire to meet soon with others of the elect body of believers. It is almost as though he is telling them that they don't have long to wait. In the context of the Tribulation, that would amount to about two more years.

The letter ends with a cryptic reference to *"thy elect sister."* Who might she be? If the elect lady is a reference to Israel in the Tribulation, why wouldn't this be a reference to Gentiles? They are, after all, brought into the family by adoption. They are the Gentile saints who have entered into the family by the witness of Israel's elect, who are at this time preaching the Gospel throughout the world. Interestingly, the very next letter seems to be addressed to them!

Year Six of the Tribulation Period as Described by the Third Epistle of John

This letter is addressed simply to *"Gaius."* It is a Latin name meaning, "rejoicing." Its entire message seems to be to the *"elect sister,"* of the previous epistle—namely, Gentile converts during the Tribulation Period.

This is borne out by the fact that the other two names addressed in the letter have their origins in pagan Gentile worship. Diotrephes (Zeus-nursed) and Demetrius (of Demeter) are names that summon up the history of demigods and goddesses. Zeus was king of the Greek gods and Demeter was a fertility goddess.

Yet, two of the three Gentiles mentioned here are commended for their faith. By implication, Gaius is shown to be one of the children who *"walk in truth."* Demetrius *"hath a good report of all men."*

By contrast, Diotrephes rejects John as an authority. By inference, he also rejects the teaching of the Apostles, which is the Church's only defense. Diotrephes has fallen prey to the temptation that it's more comfortable to join with the enemy than to fight him.

The concluding verse of this epistle is remarkably like the one in the preceding letter:

"But I trust I shall shortly see thee, and we shall speak face to face. Peace be to thee. Our friends salute thee. Greet the friends by name" (John 14).

John is now giving the Gentiles the same encouragement that he gave the Jews. He assures them that he will soon see them in person. As we draw closer to the seventh year of the Tribulation, this is precisely the message that we would expect, given the return of the Lord in glory with the armies of heaven. In these two epistles, John has sent notes of reassurance to both the Jewish and Gentile Tribulation saints.

Year Seven of the Tribulation Period as Described by the Epistle of Jude

Significantly enough, the theme of this epistle is that one should *"contend for the faith"* (Jude 3). Fighting for the Gospel and doing battle against its enemies becomes the central feature of the letter. The objects of this battle are latter-day false teachers.

It is addressed to *"them that are sanctified by God the Father, and preserved in Jesus Christ, and called"* (Jude 1). In other words, the days are difficult and Jude is reminding the recipients of the letter that the saving grace of God will bring them through to the end.

And indeed, the end is in sight here. In verses 5-7, Jude recalls the judgment of the angels that sinned, of Sodom and Gomorrah, and the Egyptians during the Exodus. In verses 8-13, he delivers a scathing denunciation of their motives and behavior.

And then, in a prophetic vision, he foresees their destruction. His pronouncement of doom includes a prophecy that goes all the way back to the beginning of Genesis:

"And Enoch also, the seventh from Adam, prophesied of these, saying, Behold, the Lord cometh with ten thousands of his saints.

"To execute judgment upon all, and to convince all that are ungodly among them of all their ungodly deeds which they have ungodly committed, and of all their hard speeches which ungodly sinners have spoken against him" (Jude 14-15).

We are now nearing the conclusion of seven years of God's wrath. How significant it is that these verses prophesy the return of the Lord as the period draws to an end. The nineteenth chapter of Revelation features a detailed look at this event. The returning Lord and His army do battle with the beast, the kings of the earth, and their armies. Satan is bound and the Lord has returned to reign triumphant. As we shall see, this theme is restated in the last two verses of the epistle.

Verses 17-23 once again urge believers to build a strong defense against false teachers. At the same time, it exhorts them to witness with renewed vigor, "pulling them out of the fire." And why not? With the late hour of the Tribulation in view, very little time will remain to save those whom the Lord has called.

The concluding doxology of Jude is one of the most beautiful in all Scripture. Significantly, it refers to the Second Coming of Christ in glory:

"Now unto him that is able to keep you from falling, and to present you faultless before the presence of his

glory with exceeding joy,
"To the only wise God our Saviour, be glory and
majesty, dominion and power, both now and ever.
Amen" (Jude 24-25).

In these last words before the Revelation of
Jesus Christ, Jude urges the brethren to fight the
good fight against apostasy. And he prophesies
the Second Coming of Christ.

Remarkably, it seems that these seven letters
provide a sort of prophetic overview of the conditions that will prevail during the great Tribulation. They seem destined to give direction, aid,
and comfort. James addresses events that launch
the Tribulation. I Peter prepares the Jew for
suffering. II Peter tells of false teachers, end-time
mockery and the prophecy of the *"day of the Lord."*
I John—the center light of this Hanukkah menorah—says:

*"This then is the message which we have heard of him,
and declare unto you, that **God is light**, and in him is
no darkness at all"* (I John 1:5).

His little children are urged to walk in the light
and to fight effectively against the wiles of the
antichrist. II and III John provide a message of
comfort and hope, first to the Jews, then to the
Gentiles under tribulation. And finally, Jude announces Christ's Second Coming, to destroy the
ungodly and to set up His kingdom.

This general view of the Tribulation is remarkable for the clear view it gives of the spiritual landscape that will prevail during the Tribulation Period.

Again, we must emphasize that the practical application of these epistles is emphatically meant for all believers. But what an incredible prophetic view they also give of the Tribulation Period. They appear to be an introduction to the following book—*The Revelation of Jesus Christ.* The entire message of Revelation revolves around seven years of judgment—concluding with the return of Christ.

The Book of Revelation

Revelation was designed as a series of menorahs—and the opening chapter shows Jesus standing on the Servant Lamp as the main character of the book. Unlike the New Testament's design, the menorahs of Revelation are not Hanukkah menorahs. They are represented by seven lamps each. I think the reason for these seven-lamp menorahs is that the Tribulation Period takes us back to the seventieth week of Daniel—an era of Law that preceded the dispensation of Grace and the institution of the Hanukkah design of the New Testament.

Because the book of Revelation reverts back to seven-lamp menorahs, I am convinced that Gentile Christianity will have been raptured into heaven before the events of the Tribulation Period commence. Revelation presents a picture of the saints in heaven and Israel struggling on earth. In the opening chapter, Jesus is seen standing on the Servant Lamp.

> *"And I turned to see the voice that spake with me. And being turned, I saw seven golden candlesticks;*
>
> *"And in the midst of the seven candlesticks one like unto the Son of man ...*
>
> *"... his eyes were as a **flame of fire**;*
>
> *"And his feet like unto fine brass, as if they **burned** in a furnace ...*
>
> *"... his countenance was **as the sun shineth** in his strength"* (Revelation 1:12-16).

A view of Jesus *"in the midst"* of seven golden lamps, actually presents Him as the *"Shamash."* The Greek account portrays Him in the Middle—as the Servant Lamp of the menorah. This concept introduces a menorah design which continues throughout the entire book of Revelation. We have determined that there are nine menorahs governing the structure of the book.

Revelation 1-7

The first seven chapters in Revelation form a menorah. In chapter 4, which takes the position of the Servant Lamp, we are given a view of the throne of God with a *"rainbow round about the throne, in sight like unto an emerald"* (Revelation 4:3).

This green rainbow is interesting. There are seven colors in the visible light spectrum—red on the lower end, blue on the high end, and green in the middle. This may be compared to the seven lamps of the menorah with the green light acting as a Servant Lamp. Green light, mixed with equal intensities of red and blue, produces white light. For example, the screen of a color television set is made up of tiny red, green, and blue lights. Together, they can produce any color in the spectrum. In like manner, it took Jesus to bring man and God together and produce righteousness.

The World Book Encyclopedia lists the religious significance of the color green as "the hope of eternal life."[1]

In the Mosaic Tabernacle, the predominant colors are red and blue. Red represents man (the name Adam means "red") and blue represents heaven. However, no green color is apparent in the Tabernacle. Perhaps it is because the Law could not forgive sins. The Law was only a school master—a teaching tool to point us to Christ. It took the green of the Messiah to bring the red of man and the blue of God together to produce the white of righteousness. There is so much that could be said about the religious significance of the colors, but at least we have demonstrated that the seven colors of the light spectrum form a menorah.

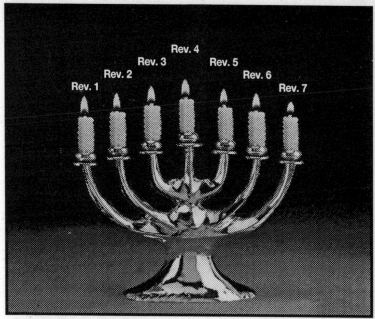

Revelation 1-7 forms the framework of a menorah. Plus, within those seven chapters are two other menorahs—the seven letters and the seven seals. Chapter 4 serves as the Shamash.

Also seen before the throne in Revelation 4 is a set of *"... seven lamps of fire burning before the throne, which are the seven Spirits of God"* (Revelation 4:5).

Menorahs in Menorahs

The first seven chapters of Revelation not only form one menorah, we also have another menorah in the first three chapters (1-3), namely the seven churches, and yet another menorah in the remaining three chapters (5-7), namely the Seven Seals.

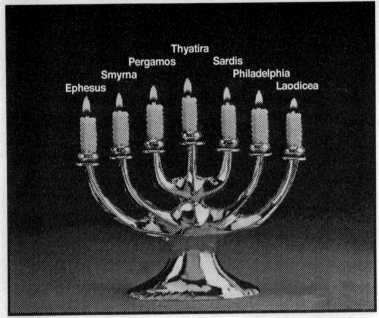

Seven letters to the churches form the framework of a menorah, with Thyatira in the middle. The message to Thyatira points to the Servant Lamp as noted below.

The Seven Churches

The Seven Churches are described as a menorah. Jesus told John that the *"seven candlesticks which thou sawest are the seven churches"* (Revelation 1:20).

To Ephesus, Jesus threatened to *"remove thy candlestick"* (Revelation 2:5).

The fourth message—to Thyatira—has a reference to the Servant Lamp: *"These things saith the Son of God, who hath his eyes like unto a flame of fire, and his feet are like fine brass"* (Rev. 2:18).

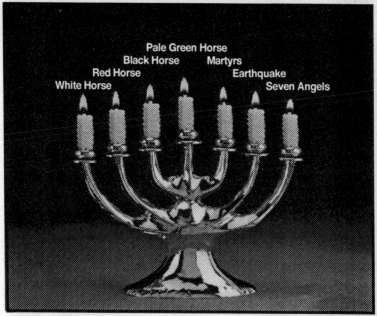

The seven seals form the framework of a third menorah. All three are viewed in the first seven chapters of Revelation. The seventh seal in Revelation 8 opens to three more menorahs.

Seven Seals

The Seven Seals form a third menorah. The fourth Seal corresponds with the Servant Lamp. In it, we are shown a *"pale"* horse. First of all, it is pale as opposed to bright. It appears to be produced, not from light emmiters, but from light absorbing materials. Secondly, the Greek word translated *"pale"* is "chlorus"—from which we get the word chlorophyll. Its color is pale green—similar, but not like the bright green rainbow around the throne of God.

At this point, I would like to discuss the subject of colors again. I think of this green as Satan's counterfeit source—as if he was not using light emitters, but light absorbing materials. It is as if Satan's color is yellow. Pale green is produced by mixing yellow and blue paints. Light absorbing colors produce negative effects, whereas mixing colors of light produces positive effects. Evidently, Lucifer, whose name means "light bearer," can only reflect the light of another source. He is not a source of light within himself. He is the ruler of the darkness of this world. Jesus, on the other hand, is seen in Revelation 1:16 as a light source—with a countenance that appears *"as the sun shineth in his strength."*

For example, mixing equal intensities of red, green, and blue light produces white light. But mixing equal amounts of red, yellow, and blue paint produces black paint. Green light acts as a catalyst or Servant Lamp among the light emmiters, while yellow paint acts as a catalyst or Servant Lamp among light absorbing materials. These positive and negative aspects of colors serve to illustrate the conflict between good and evil. In the Bible, light is used as a metaphor for good, while darkness is used as a metaphor for evil. Paul used such a metaphor as he told King Agrippa that he was sent, *"... to open their eyes, and to turn them from* **darkness** *to* **light**, *and from the power of Satan unto God ..."* (Acts 26:18).

Revelation 8-14 forms another menorah, which features the two witnesses in Chapter 11 as its Servant Lamp. Two other menorahs also appear, seven trumpets and seven personages.

Revelation 8-14

The book of Revelation has 22 chapters. And, believe it or not, there are three major divisions. As we have just discussed, the first seven chapters (1-7) form a menorah; the next seven chapters (8-14) form a second menorah; while the remaining chapters form a third menorah. The Servant Lamp this second menorah may be observed in the middle chapter (11). Revelation 11:4 says, *"These are the two olive trees, and the two **candlesticks** standing before the God of the earth."*

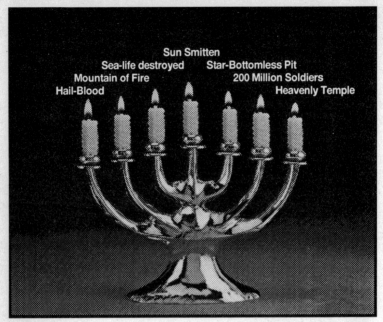

Within the framework of Rev. 8-14 is yet another lampstand, which may be viewed in the form of seven trumpets. The fourth trumpet affects the Servant Lamp of our universe—the sun.

What can I say? It couldn't be any clearer! The two witnesses correspond to the lamps of the menorah—making chapter 11 a Servant Lamp for the seven chapters of Revelation 8-14.

Seven Trumpets

On one side of this menorah of Revelation 8-14, we have Seven Trumpets which form another menorah. The fourth trumpet corresponds to a Servant Lamp: *"The fourth angel sounded, and the third part of the **sun** was smitten"* (Revelation 8:12)! Yes, the fourth trumpet affects the light of the great Servant Lamp of our universe—the sun!

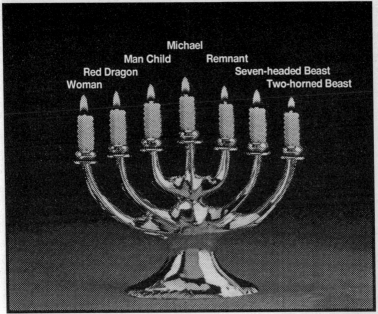

Michael
Man Child   Remnant
Red Dragon   Seven-headed Beast
Woman   Two-horned Beast

Seven personages in Revelation 12-14 reveal a sixth menorah with the conflict between Michael and Satan forming the center position.

Seven Personages

On the other side of the menorah of Revelation 8-14, are Seven Personages, representing a sixth menorah! The fourth character corresponds to a Servant Lamp. It is Michael who fights the devil and throws him out of heaven.

This is the continuing conflict between good and evil—which, by the way, is the very essence of the mystery of the Menorah. Lucifer, whose name means "the light bearer," wanted to be equal with God.

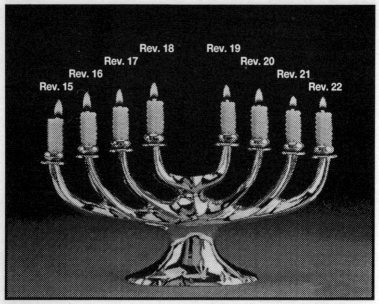

Rev. 18   Rev. 19
Rev. 17   Rev. 20
Rev. 16   Rev. 21
Rev. 15   Rev. 22

Revelation 15-22 forms the third major division of the prophecy. This time an eighth lamp has been added. The destruction of Mystery Babylon and the return of Christ take center stage in what we consider to be the conflict of the Servant Lamps.

Revelation 15-22

The concluding chapters of Revelation (15-22) reflect a third major menorah in the structure of the book. In this case we have eight chapters. In the two central chapters (18-19) there is a competition between Mystery Babylon and Christ for the position of Servant Lamp—and in chapter 19, Christ wins! In chapter 18, we see the destruction of Mystery Babylon. In verse 18, we are told that the merchants of earth *"cried when they saw the smoke of her burning."* And in verse 23, God says, *"And the **light of a candle***

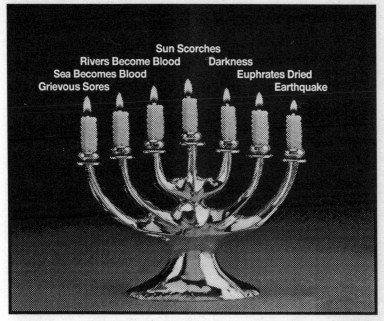

Sun Scorches
Rivers Become Blood   Darkness
Sea Becomes Blood   Euphrates Dried
Grievous Sores   Earthquake

Within the framework of this final menorah is another menorah—seven vials of God's wrath. The center or fourth vial affects the Sun, just as we saw in the fourth trumpet.

shall shine no more at all in thee!" In Chapter 19, we see the winning Servant Lamp as He returns to earth with power and great glory!

Seven Vials

In one side of this menorah (15-17) we have Seven Vials of wrath—which form yet another menorah. The Servant Lamp is seen in the fourth vial: *"And the fourth angel poured out his vial upon the **sun:** and power was given unto him to scorch men with fire"* (Revelation 16:8).

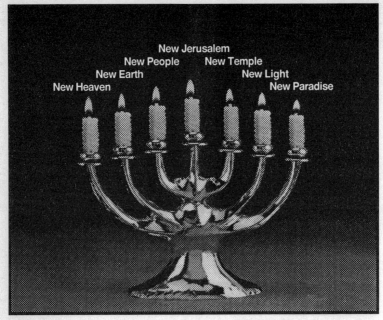

New Jerusalem
New People   New Temple
New Earth   New Light
New Heaven   New Paradise

Concluding the book of Revelation is a menorah of seven new things. The Servant Lamp is represented by the Holy city, New Jerusalem, which has no need of the sun!

Seven New Things

On the other side of this menorah (19-22) we have yet another menorah—seven new things. The fourth new thing corresponds to the Servant Lamp. It is the NEW JERUSALEM!

> "Having the **glory** of God and her **light** was like unto a stone most precious.
> "And the city has no need of the sun, neither of the moon, to shine in it: for the glory of God did lighten it, and the Lamb is the **light** thereof" (Revelation 21:11,23).

Did you ever see a book designed so brilliantly

(pardon the pun) as the design of the book of Revelation? No mere man could have designed the book to represent so many menorahs layered upon menorahs—and the theme of the book is Jesus, the Servant Lamp—who was snuffed out on the day he died, only to rise again!

Count them. Revelation has "nine" menorahs— thus making a magnificent Hanukkah menorah to climax and close out God's great plan of the ages! The menorah design of the book of Revelation is obvious. It says to me that it is a Jewish book—written to describe the concluding events predicted by Jewish prophets of old. The nine menorahs of seven lamps each implies that the book describes the final transition from the old "sevens" of Law to the "nines" of Grace.

The Hebrew *Aleph-beit*

While researching this mystery of the Menorah, we came across an equally astounding discovery, which we would like to share with you. The theme of each of the 22 chapters of Revelation correspond to the meanings of each of the 22 letters of the Hebrew *Aleph-beit*. Please read on!

Chapter Four Note:

1. World Book Encyclopedia, Volume 4, page 664.

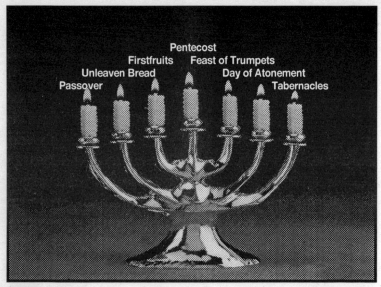

The Jewish Holy Days follow a menorah design—with Pentecost as the Servant Lamp.

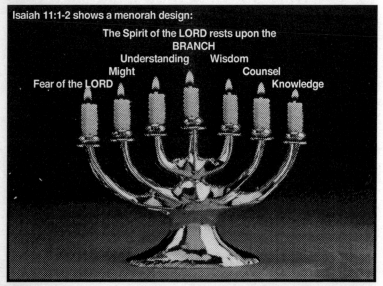

Isaiah 11:1-2 gives the seven attributes of the Spirit upon the Messiah—the Branch that grows out of the root of Jesse.

Chapter Five

Revelation and the Hebrew *Aleph-beit*

As has often been observed, the book of Revelation is comprised of themes that are essentially Jewish. We acknowledge, of course, that its first three chapters have been considered a prophetic profile of the historical Church Age. But the majority of the book—chapters 4 through 20—is devoted to that future period designated as *"the time of Jacob's trouble"* (Jeremiah 30:7). These chapters involve the Jews who will endure the Great Tribulation.

Revelation also heralds the Second Coming of Christ with the introduction of the Kingdom Age and its final resolution, as God brings the writings of the ancient Jewish prophets to reality. It is in Revelation that 144,000 from the twelve tribes of Israel are sealed for God's service. They are made leaders in the restorative work of God.

The prophet Jeremiah not only gives the Tribulation a title—*"the time of **Jacob's** trouble"*—but clearly states the reason for God's wrath during this time. The Jews will suffer *"Jacob's trouble"* in order to be exalted. In this process, order and justice will be re-established in the world.

In Jeremiah 31:31, we are given the central aspect of Israel's final restoration to their Promised Land, as Jerusalem becomes the political center of the world:

> *"Behold, the days come, saith the Lord, that I will make a **new covenant** with the house of Israel, and with the house of Judah."*

The process of delivering this *"new covenant"* to Israel is detailed in the book of Revelation. It begins with the opening of seven seals in chapter 6. Then, in chapter 7, the Jews are directly dealt with:

> *"And I heard the number of them which were sealed: and there were sealed **an hundred and forty and four thousand** of all the tribes of the children of Israel."*

Here, in verse 4, the righteous remnant is both commissioned for the work they must do, and protected from the horrible conditions under which they will labor during the Tribulation. Later, in chapter 14, the Jews will *"follow the Lamb whithersoever he goeth"* (Revelation 14:4).

The Revelation Narrative

With Israel at the center of activity in Revelation, it should come as no surprise that we would discover aspects of Jewish doctrine in the pattern of its written narrative. As we have already noted, the appearance of the Jewish Menorah stands with startling clarity among the sevens that so clearly characterize this book.

Biblical commentators have noted that the menorahs of the Tabernacle and Temple symbolized and foreshadowed the person of Christ.

But, for the Jews, the Menorah is an important national symbol, appearing on Israeli currency and official documents. Its unveiling as a New Testament symbol must ultimately have a moving effect upon Jewish scholars.

Seven Is No Longer Just a Number

We have also demonstrated that Jesus is the center lamp among the seven lights of the Menorah. He is typified in the *Shamash*, or Servant Candle, who provides the flame from which the entire lampstand is lit. In the Menorah, the light of Jesus is always the prominent feature of the center—or fourth—member.

But that study led to another investigation in which a surprising concept sprang to life. As with the case of the Menorah, its effect upon Jewish thinking will also be profound. What follows is an explanation of the marvelous relation between the Hebrew *Aleph-beit* and the book of Revelation.

The "Word" and His Letters

Revelation 1:13 graphically depicts Jesus as the Servant Candle:

> *"And in the midst of the seven candlesticks one like unto the son of man, clothed with a garment down to the foot, and girt about the paps with a golden girdle."*

But it is also true that four times, in Revelation 1:8, 1:11, 21:6 and 22:13, Jesus says, *I am Alpha and Omega."*

These are the first and last letters in the Greek Alphabet. It seems rather obvious that if Jesus refers to Himself in this way, He must intend for us to see that He is also represented by all the letters between Alpha and Omega—in other words, the entire Alphabet.

Since we already know Him as the *"Word"* (John 1:1), and words are made up of letters, it is perfectly natural that He would depict himself in this way. Remarkably, we find that His statement links the Greek Alphabet with the Hebrew *Aleph-beit* of the Old Testament. Christ is not just the *"Alpha and Omega,"* He is the א *aleph* and the ת *tahv.*

The Old Testament *Aleph-beit*

John's Gospel makes it clear that Jesus was the *"Word"* long before His incarnation. Therefore, in ancient days, when Old Testament Scripture was being written, He must have borne the same relationship to its inspired language.

This observation leads to yet another pertinent Jewish teaching. It is the concept of the **"word,"** which is said by rabbinical teaching to characterize God's creative power.

In Romans 3:1-3, Paul writes:

> *"What advantage hath the Jew? or what profit is there of circumcision?*
> *"Much every way: chiefly, because that unto them were committed the oracles of God."*

Here is a great truth. The ancient prophets were especially equipped by God to receive and preserve His Word.

In Romans 11:12, Paul makes yet another point about the Jews:

> *"Now if the fall of them be the riches of the world, and the diminishing of them the riches of the Gentiles; how much more their fullness?"*

In other words, the Jews are keepers of a great deal of Scriptural truth that has blessed the Gentiles, and will continue to do so with increasing effect in the future, as Israel rises to power.

One such truth is the spiritual imagery of the
Hebrew *Aleph-beit*. For centuries, they have
taught that its 22 letters contain 22 messages of
deep spiritual meaning.

Researching the menorahs (sevens) in Revelation, we were taken with the fact that the letters
of the Hebrew *Aleph-beit* bear an uncanny correspondence to the 22 chapters of Revelation. Each
letter and its meaning corresponds to the theme
of each chapter—more than a mere coincidence.

The Hebrew text of the Old Testament corre-
lates perfectly with the meaning of the New
Testament Alpha and Omega. It is as if the book
of Revelation was actually written for the Jews!

If, in the New Testament, Jesus is characterized
as the first and last letters of the Greek Alphabet,
then it is reasonable to assume that He must also
be visible in the first and last letters of the
Hebrew *Aleph-beit*—the language of the Old Testament. This idea is beautifully illustrated in
Genesis 1:1, the first sentence of the Bible.

We have already noted that Genesis 1:1 contains seven Hebrew words—a menorah in itself.
The word in the center—or fourth—position is
spelled with the first and last letters of the Hebrew
Aleph-beit, namely the א *aleph* and the ת *tahv*,
corresponding to the *"Alpha and Omega"* of the
Greek language. Jesus, as the *"Word"* is literally

positioned in the first sentence of the Bible! Moreover, He occupies the position of the *Shamash*, or Servant Candle—at the center of a menorah.

Even if you don't read Hebrew, the following illustration clearly shows how this works:

בראשית ברא אלהים **את** השמים ואת הארץ:

ha'aretz · va'eht · hashamayim · **eht** · Elohim · barah · bereshit

Genesis 1:1, with its seven Hebrew words. Note the *aleph* and the *tahv* in the center (or fourth) "Servant Candle" position.

This phenomenon clearly demonstrates the continuity of Scripture. John 1:3 says, *"All things were made by him...."* The Word was the force of creation, and His signature appears in Genesis 1:1. There, as in Revelation, He stands in the midst of a menorah (see page 29).

The Hebrew *Aleph-beit*

But the idea of the creative force of the *"Word"* is also a Jewish concept.

For centuries, Jewish sages have taught that the Hebrew *Aleph-beit* is descended from the original letters given by God to man. As such, they are not merely accidental shapes, but conform to a system of wisdom. Writing in *"The Wisdom in the Hebrew Alphabet,"* Rabbi Michael L. Munk says,

"The twenty-two sacred letters are profound, primal spiritual forces. They are in effect, the raw material of Creation. When God combined them into words, phrases, commands, they brought about Creation, translating His will into reality, as it were.... Just as the 'word of God' gave being to heaven, so it is His word that gives being to everything."[1]

As Christians, we know that the *"Word"* is more than a mere collection of letters, no matter how powerful. He is a person, who incorporates the power of God's creation into the whole of His character:

*"In the beginning was the **Word**, and the **Word** was with God, and the **Word** was God.*
"The same was in the beginning with God.
"All things were made by him; and without him was not any thing made that was made" (John. 1:1-3).

In these first three verses from the Gospel of John, we see the clear actions of the "Word of Creation."

From a Jewish perspective, minus its personhood, the *"Word"* is an Alphabet that has a kind of power of its own, since God used it to command creation. Picking up this idea, Rabbi Munk has compiled a systematic teaching, based upon centuries of commentaries. Quotes regarding the meaning of the Hebrew *Aleph-beit*, unless otherwise noted, are taken from his book.

With regard to Genesis 1:1, and its את *aleph-tahv*, he says, "This usage alludes to the fact that the universe was created in complete perfection, 'from *aleph* to *tahv*.'" The א *aleph* and ת *tahv* encompass the entire Hebrew *Aleph-beit*.

Rabbinic teaching says that the Word not only created everything, but continues to hold it together. Rabbi Munk writes,

> "The heaven continues to exist because not an instant goes by without God continuing to say, in effect 'let there be a firmament'—otherwise they would return to the status that prevailed before God's will was uttered. So it is with every aspect of Creation. God's original Ten Utterances are repeated constantly in the sense that the divine will of the original six days remains in force. Otherwise, everything would revert to the nothingness of before Creation."[2]

His words remind us of the verse in the letter to the Hebrews [1:3], where Christ is said to be *"upholding all things by the word of his power."* Here, the *"Word,"* in addition to being the force of creation, is also the energy of continuance. His constant activity holds the creation together.

An Abecedary of 22 Chapters

An abecedary is a literary structure in which sections of the writing are connected with the letters of the alphabet in their regular order. A well-known example would be, "A is for Apple, B is for Ball, C is for Cat ... etc." In like manner, the Hebrew *Aleph-beit* appears to offer a similar literary structure. Jewish teaching holds that each of the 22 letters of the Hebrew *Aleph-beit* carries with it a certain complex of meanings. How these meanings were derived is not always certain. Some of them seem to emanate from the letter's shape. Others come from word association, numerical designation or the letter's sound. But, however these meanings originated, one thing is certain: the teaching has been fixed and formalized. The meanings of the letters do not shift.

That's why it is extremely curious that the symbolism given by Jewish teachers to each letter seems to relate—sometimes with amazing clarity—to its corresponding chapter in the book of Revelation. These 22 chapters may, in fact, be a sort of abecedary in which the "*Word*" is separated into His component letters.

Let's begin by looking at the Hebrew letters one by one. First comes the letter א *aleph*. Following it, and each succeeding Hebrew letter, will be a general statement of its Jewish meaning and symbolism. This will be compared, in turn, with the major message of each chapter in the book of Revelation.

Revelation, Chapter One

The ℵ *aleph*, first letter of the Hebrew *Aleph-beit*, represents the number one. Each Hebrew letter, in fact, has a numerical value and may also be used as a numeral.

According to Rabbi Munk, ℵ *aleph* symbolizes the "One and Only, the Eternal, the Omnipotent God."[3] It is said to be the master letter, proclaiming both the name of God and His divinity. It is the link between heaven and earth; between God and the finite physical creation.

For Christians, the number one has always had a similar meaning. It is perhaps best expressed in Ephesians 4:4-6:

> *"There is* **one** *body, and* **one** *Spirit, even as ye are called in* **one** *hope of your calling;*
> *"***One** *Lord,* **one** *faith,* **one** *baptism,*
> *"***One** *God and Father of all, who is above all, and through all, and in you all."*

This sevenfold statement declares the concept, meaning, and value of the number one.

The first chapter of Revelation features this very same picture, as John writes in verse 8:

*"I am Alpha and Omega, the beginning and the
ending, saith the Lord, which is , and which was, and
which is to come, the Almighty."*

The ascended Lord is revealed in verse 8 as the
Lord God Almighty. He is One and Eternal. He is
the link between heaven and earth.

In verse 18, Christ declares, *"I am he that liveth,
and was dead; and, behold, I am alive for ever-
more, Amen."* This is an absolutely incredible
statement—especially in the light of the meaning
of א *aleph*, the first letter of the Hebrew *Aleph-
beit.*

As we approach chapter 2 and the spiritual
significance of the letter ב *beit*, let us note that the
message of Christ is directed toward the seven
churches, as they are issued a call to action, in
order to bring about His prophetic plan.

Revelation, Chapter Two

The letter ב *beit* is said to be the number of blessing and creation—of beginning. *Baruch,* the Hebrew word for blessing, begins with ב *beit*. The first two Hebrew words of Genesis 1:1 also begin with this letter. *Bereshit barah Elohim* ... are translated into English as, *"Bereshit* [In the beginning]; *barah* [created]; *Elohim* [God] ..."

The ב *beit*, having the value of "two," is also said to be the letter of duality; good versus evil and right versus wrong, the curse of disobedience that accompanies the blessing of obedience.

Many Christian expositors have also taught that two is the number of division, opposition, or enmity.

Significantly, Jews declare ב *beit* to be the number of the home, the house of meeting, or the Holy Temple, since the very pronunciation of this letter forms the Hebrew word that means "house."

How appropriate it is, then, to observe that the second chapter of Revelation is addressed to the first four of seven churches in Asia Minor. Each of them is a house of meeting—a geographical location that typifies the life and work of the Church.

Perfectly matching the declared meaning of ב *beit,* the Lord pronounces a blessing for obedience and a curse for disobedience upon each of these houses of meeting.

Note that the four churches mentioned in this chapter picture the beginning of the Church Age. *Beit* is the letter of beginning.

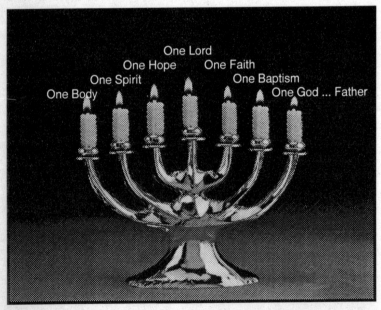

Ephesians 4:4-6 gives a seven-fold statement of the importance of the number "one" (see page 119). The menorah design is obvious: *Hope* and *Faith* flank on either side of *Lord* (the Servant Lamp); *Spirit* and *Baptism* correspond; etc.

Revelation, Chapter Three

The ג *gimel*, third letter of the Hebrew *Aleph-beit*, is also used as the number three. It is said to be "the symbol of kindness and culmination." The ג *gimel* "is cognate to *gamol*, which means to nourish until completely ripe."[4] We can see both "kindness" (as in Philadelphia) and  "culmination" (as in Laodicea) depicted in Revelation, chapter 3.

First, the ג *gimel* represents God's loving-kindness and goodness. In response to these qualities, the spiritual man must attempt to reflect them in his life. In like manner, the Philadelphian church is the most desirable of the churches in this chapter, and is said to represent precisely these qualities. From the translation of its name, it is commonly said to be the church of "brotherly love." In this respect, the message of ג *gimel* fits perfectly.

Secondly, Revelation 3 speaks of the culmination of the Church Age under the nurture of the Holy Spirit. This ripening of the Church brings to mind the parable of Jesus, in which He likened the kingdom of heaven to seed planted in a field.

When weeds planted by the enemy are said to be growing up with the good wheat, Jesus concludes:

> *"Let both grow together until the harvest: and in the time of harvest I will say to the reapers, Gather ye together first the tares, and bind them in bundles to burn them: but gather the wheat into my barn"* (Matthew 13:30).

Also, Christian expositors have often noted that the number three denotes the Godhead and, by implication, entirety or fullness. In like manner, this chapter brings the Church Age to culmination—its "entirety or fullness."

Chapter 3 concludes with the picture of Jesus standing at the door and knocking to be allowed entrance into the life of the man of faith—which brings us to the next letter, ד *dalet*. Furthermore, the next chapter begins with this same image—a door!

Revelation, Chapter Four

The letter ד *dalet* is the number four. It is cognate with the Hebrew, *delet*, "door." "The ד *dalet* also alludes to *dahl*, pauper, who knocks on doors begging for alms ... The shape of the ד *dalet* is like that of a door with its lintel spreading right and left, and its doorpost reaching up and down."[5]

What a strange "coincidence" it is, then, to look at Revelation 4 and see in verse 1:

> *"After this I looked, and, behold, a **door** was opened in heaven: and the first voice which I heard was as it were of a trumpet talking with me; which said, Come up hither, and I will shew thee things which must be hereafter."*

Revelation 3 ended with Christ knocking on a door. Chapter 4 opens with the forceful image of a door that allows access to heaven.

The number 4 (ד *dalet*) represents the material creation with its four divisions of the day, four seasons, four tides, four cardinal directions and four phases of the moon, as well as the attributes of God's creativity.

In Genesis 10:5, men were divided according to

four designations: "... *lands ... tongues ... families ... nations.*" Thus, four has been called the number of the kingdom.

In this chapter of Revelation, we see God's throne—symbol of the kingdom. This chapter launches the end-time events that culminate in the reign of Christ as King of kings—in perfect harmony with the meaning of *dalet* and its corresponding number four.

The royal throne is accompanied by the seven lamps that represent God's Holy Spirit. But we also see the four beasts, or living creatures, which are representatives of—or watchers over—the material creation:

> *"And before the throne was a sea of glass like unto crystal: and in the midst of the throne, and round about the throne, were* **four** *beasts full of eyes before and behind"* (v. 6).

Here, we see a picture of divine action. It is directed toward planet earth—God's material creation. The kingdom is about to be established.

Revelation, Chapter Five

To the Jews, the ה *hay*, with its numerical value of five, is symbolic of the divine name of God. In Hebrew writings, ה *hay* is an abbreviation for God. It is associated with repentance and mercy. The Hebrew word *teshuvah*, meaning "repentance," can be separated into  two parts: *teshuv*, followed by ה *hay*. In this case, the rabbis say it becomes, *teshuv* (return to) *hay* (God). This "return to God" is a prominent feature of Revelation, chapter 5, where the drama commences.

In his commentary on ה *hay*, Rabbi Munk writes,

"The Passover Haggadah [story] speaks of two **new songs** of rejoicing, one in the feminine form [*shirah chadashah*] and one in the masculine [*shir chadash*]. We introduce *Hallel*, the psalms [113-118] of praise for the Exodus, by calling it *shirah chadashah*, a **new song**, spelled with the feminine suffix *hay*. The song of Messianic Day, however, is described as *shir chadash*, in the masculine form. Before *Hallel*, when we are about to thank God for redeeming us from the Egyptian bondage, we use the feminine form to suggest that the redemption was incomplete, as it was followed by other exiles and sufferings, each more painful than the preceding one. This as yet unended chain of national suffering is similar to labor pangs which ease up for a short period only to be followed by more severe pain. Indeed, the tribulations of Israel are called the birthpangs of the Messiah."[6]

This commentary on ה *hay*, is filled with some profound insights which are necessary to address at this point. First we note that a masculine *"new song"* is given in this very chapter which corresponds to the feminine letter ה *hay*:

> *"And they sung a **new song**, saying, Thou are worthy to take the book, and to open the seals thereof: for thou wast slain, and has redeemed us to God by thy blood out of every kindred, and tongue, and people and nation"* (Revelation 5:9).

This *"new song"* appears to be the *shir chadash* (masculine form)—the song of the Messianic Day. Yet, it is found in the chapter that corresponds to the feminine ה *hay*. It fits, however, because this "incomplete redemption" begins its final process in this chapter. The Lamb takes the scroll!

According to Rabbi Munk, there are two "new songs"—one feminine and one masculine. The feminine song (shirah) was composed following the Exodus out of Egypt. It is found in Psalms 113-118 and is recited several times a year in synagogues. It commemorates the Exodus. It is called a *shirah* (feminine form) because it represents something incomplete. Rabbi Munk said the future *"new song"* will be sung in the Messianic Day.

In accordance with this concept, the Song of Moses was called a *shirah* (incomplete feminine form). It is a prophetic riddle, most of which has yet to be fulfilled. On the other hand, the Song of the Lamb which begins in Revelation 5, is a masculine *shir*. It is the *"new song"* which Jews have looked forward to singing down through their years of suffering.

In Revelation 14:3, some 144,000 Jews sing this predicted *"new song."* It must be that *shir chadash* which the rabbis have looked forward to singing. Note that these 144,000 Jews are called "virgins." Verse 4 says, *"These are they which were not defiled with women."* Could this be a reference to that future generation far removed from those who had to sing the incomplete feminine Egyptian Hallel—the *shirah chadashah?* The song they sing is the Song of the Lamb. Only they can sing it because, *"these are they which follow the Lamb, whithersoever he goeth."* The song they sing is the *shir chadash!*

In Revelation 15:3, as the Tribulation nears a close and the work of redemption for Israel is nearly complete, the saints in heaven sing two songs—the song of Moses and the song of the Lamb:

> *"And I saw as it were a sea of glass mingled with fire: and them that had gotten the victory over the beast, and over his image, and over his mark, and over the number*

*of his name, stand on the sea of glass, having the harps
of God.*

*"And they sing the song of Moses, the servant of God,
and the song of the Lamb, saying, Great and marvelous
are thy works, Lord God Almighty; just and true are thy
ways, thou King of saints.*

*"Who shall not fear thee, O Lord, and glorify thy
name: for thou only art holy: for all nations shall come
and worship before thee; for thy judgments are made
manifest"* (Revelation 15:2-4).

Both the song of Moses *(shirah chadashah)* and
the song of the Lamb *(shir chadash)* are sung
together. The redemption is finally being completed!

In Revelation 5, the Lamb of God is found
worthy to take the book and begin the final
process of redemption, which will establish His
throne and His people, Israel. In the process,
Judaism will return to Him.

To Gentile Christianity, five is the number of
grace. Here, God turns His attention from the
redeemed church age and begins the process of
bringing about Israel's glorious redemption. Even
today, rabbis are calling for repentance that redemption might come.

Revelation, Chapter Six

The ו *vav* has a gematria (numerical value) of six. According to rabbinic commentary, it denotes physical completion, redemption, and transformation:

> "The physical world was completed in six days and a complete self-contained object consists of six dimensions: above and below, right and left, before and behind ... The Jewish nation, too, is complete, self-contained, unique; that is why the number six is so prominent in the story of its growth to nationhood."[7]

It is generally believed that the six days of creation represent a prophecy that all things will be completed, redeemed, and transformed at the close of six thousand years. Perhaps for that reason, the apocalyptic events of completion, redemption, and transformation commence in Revelation, chapter 6 with the breaking of the seals and the opening of the scroll—title deed to earth.

Also, the letter ו *vav* "is the prefix of conjunction; it unites manifold, even opposing concepts. It is the link connecting heaven and earth. Its form is that of a hook, as indeed its name [*vav*] means 'hook.'" The ו *vav* links words and phrases to form sentences; it joins sentences into paragraphs and chapters; it connects one chapter to another; and even unites books. It may also be translated into the English word, "and."

In this chapter of Revelation, six seals are opened. As each seal is broken, the narrative begins with the conjunction "and." This is the beginning of God's wrath upon an unbelieving mankind. It is not merely an aimless outpouring of divine anger, but a systematic redemption of the earth.

E. W. Bullinger[8] stating the Christian interpretation observes that six is the number of man, his labor and his worship, true or false, since he was created on the sixth day. He notes that the serpent, too, was created on the sixth day. Therefore, this is the number of sin and the antichrist. Significantly, he is seen in verse 2 of this chapter as he rides forth, *"conquering, and to conquer."*

Revelation 13:18 emphasizes the mystical significance of six as it pertains to the great imposter:

> *"Here is wisdom. Let him that hath understanding count the number of the beast: for it is the number of a man; and his number is Six hundred three score and six."*

This man is introduced in Revelation 6!

Revelation, Chapter Seven

The ז *zayin* is said to be the letter of "spirit, sustenance and struggle." Its numerical value is seven. It is said to represent the "focal point," or center of peace. Rabbis point out that "seven comprises the six physical directions of expansion (east, west, north,  south, up, down) plus one, representing its own individual focal point." The commentary continues:

> "Figuratively, [the human] condition is likened to the six directions—east, south, west, north, up and down—that surround every human being wherever he is. The directions are the influences that work on him incessantly. They are outside of man, at a distance from his essence, but he is never free of them, always surrounded by them. The seventh factor is the placid center of it all—the inner man who is the object of all the forces, but is not a part of them. How well he succeeds in shaping and maintaining his identity in accordance with the spiritual dictates of his soul is the challenge and purpose of life."[9]

How appropriate is this image to Revelation Seven! Here, in verses 1 through 8, we have the sealing of the 144,000 from the 12 tribes of Israel, for God's service. They are caught in the midst of the most turbulent period of human history, yet they are chosen and sealed, protected so that they might carry on the work of God with perfect confidence.

In verses 9-17, we see the multitude of saints who are saved *"out of great tribulation."* They stand safe before the throne of God.

Rabbi Munk notes that the Hebrew word זַן *zahn*, beginning with the letter ז *zayin*, is the verb, "to sustain." As such, this letter "conveys to man that the Omnipotent One will assure him success in his necessary endeavors for physical survival." How important this will be to the righteous remnant in the Tribulation!

Additionally, the name זַיִן *zayin* is the Hebrew word for "weapon." It is commonly seen as a symbol of self-defense under trying conditions.

The 144,000 and their converts will surely be under great persecution, and will be forced to adopt a posture of self-defense!

Revelation, Chapter 8

About the letter ח *chet*, the Jewish commentary says:

> "Going beyond seven, the number eight symbolizes man's ability to transcend the limitations of physical existence. Thus, with a gematria, or numerical value of eight, *chet* stands for that which is on a plane above nature, i.e., the metaphysical Divine."[10]

Once again, we are startled at the correspondence between the Hebrew symbolism and the activity found in Revelation 8:1:

> *"And when he had opened the seventh seal, there was silence in heaven about the space of half an hour."*

Here, the scene has shifted to heaven—"on a plane above nature"—where we see seven angels and seven trumpets. Everyone breathlessly awaits the next event. Then, another (eighth) angel arrives with a golden censer.

He receives incense to offer, along with the prayers of the saints. His censer is then cast to earth, initiating yet another set of seven judgments. In themselves, these actions are manifestations of the Divine Nature physically touching the face of planet earth.

In this chapter, the judgments of God are linked with the incense of prayer. Here, we are reminded that it is through prayer that man transcends the limitations of physical existence!

Revelation, Chapter 9

This letter ט *tet* is something of an enigma. Its gematria is 9, but its symbolism appears contradictory, until one looks at it from the perspective of Revelation 9. Its two major meanings are, first, a serpent, and second, objective good.

The first of these meanings seems quite appropriate, since we have the blowing of the fifth and sixth judgment trumpets in this chapter. The first trumpet gives us a view of a hoard of tormenting demons from the underworld. The second trumpet produces an army of 200,000,000 *"horsemen,"* whose work is to torment unrighteous mankind. Certainly, we see the work of *"that old serpent"* in this chapter. The very shape of ט *tet* gives the appearance of a snake with its head rising on the left and its tail coiling on the right.

But what about the second meaning of ט *tet*—objective goodness? It is hard to see objective goodness in this chapter. The rabbinic commentary clarifies the view:

> "Man longs for a 'good' life, 'good' health, 'good' business, a 'good' year. But what is good? Success is often ephemeral and prosperity corrupting, while set-

backs and adversity often set the stage for advancement and triumph. Only God knows what is truly, objectively good for man."[11]

And this comment brings a great peace to the matter:

"According to the Midrash, *tet* alludes to [*tiet*], mud, and is symbolic of physical matter from which man's body was created and to which he will return ... Without faith, people could consider certain events that befall them to be as foul and unwanted as mud. However, in his awareness of God's eternal beneficence, the righteous person faithfully trusts that 'whatever the Merciful One does, He does for the best.'"

Revelation 9:19 describes the torments that will afflict the world:

"For their power is in their mouth, and in their tails: for their tails were like unto **serpents**, *and had heads, and with them they do hurt."*

In this chapter then, we see the sting of the serpent, tempered by the knowledge that behind all this horror is the objective goodness of God, as He uses these events to purify His people. It is also significant that the letter ט *tet* is said by the rabbis to represent diminishment, followed by enlargement. In like manner, the Tribulation will be followed by the Millennial reign of Christ.

Revelation, Chapter 10

In this chapter, John receives the little book from a "mighty angel." This angel stood upon dry land (Israel) and upon the (Mediterranean) sea. John was instructed to eat the little book. It seems that the scroll—sweet to the taste, but bitter in the stomach—contains the title deed to earth. It is the

scroll of chapters 5 and 6. The seals are broken and the scroll is open.

The Hebrew letter ‏י‎ *yod* stands for the number ten. It is said to represent God's creativity and His deeper spiritual realities:

> "God created the universe with the letters *yod* and *hay* which form the Divine Name, *Yah*. With the letter *yod*, He created the World to Come, while with the *hay* He created this World."[12]

Chapter 10 witnesses the angel declaring that,

> *"in the days of the voice of the seventh angel, when he shall begin to sound, the mystery of God should be finished, as he hath declared to his servants the prophets"* (Revelation 10:7).

This idea of conclusion parallels the fact that ‏י‎ *yod* represents the number ten. The rabbis teach that the number ten should be viewed as a unit.

For example, "it took ten generations from Adam to Noah to complete the breakdown of morality to such an extent that mankind—except for Noah and his family—had to be destroyed."[13]

They also say that with ten utterances, God created the world; these correspond to the Ten Commandments. Ten plagues freed the Israelites from Egypt, etc. Also, in Hebrew, both the name of God and the name of Israel begin with a ' *yod.*

The letter ' *yod* means "hand." In this chapter, it is important to note that the angel held the scroll in his hand. In verse 5, we are told that the angel lifted his hand toward heaven and *"sware ... that there should be time no longer."* The hand is a prominent part of the story related in chapter 10.

Revelation, Chapter 11

The letter כ (ך) *kaf* is the first of five Hebrew letters that can be written in two forms כ and ך. The first form כ is used when *kaf* is located at the beginning of a word or in the middle of a word. The "final form" ך is used when *kaf* is placed at the

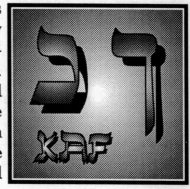

end of a word. Examples: כתר *keter* (crown); מלך *melek* (king).

The first form כ *kaf* assumes a "kneeling position" and the "final form" ך *kaf* appears to have a "standing position." It is said that the first form כ *kaf* represents the humility of the believer during this life and that the "final form" ך *kaf* shows the believer standing in his glory before God in the end time. The "final forms" are prophetic of the "end of days." There are five letters that use "final forms:"

כ (ך) *kaf*; מ (ם) *mem*; נ (ן) *nun*; פ (ף) *peh*; צ (ץ) *tzaddi*.

These five "final forms" add a prophetic dimension to the spiritual significance of the Hebrew *Aleph-beit*. As we present each of the "final forms," we will explain the prophetic concept. The "final

form" of ך *kaf* reveals the exaltation of the humble
saint in the day of judgment. Also the final form
of *kaf* denotes "possession" as in the case of בביתך
b'beitak, which means "in <u>thine</u> house" (Deut.
6:7). Note: you possess the house. On judgment
day, the saint will possess rewards.

The כ (ך) *kaf* has a numerical value of twenty. It
is said to be "the symbol of crowning accomplishment." It is the first letter of the Hebrew word,
keter, or "crown."

> "There are three crowns ... the crown of the priest-
> hood, the crown of kingship, and the crown of Torah,
> but a fourth one—the crown of a good name—is supe-
> rior to them all."[14]

How fitting it is that this chapter of Revelation
features the crowning accomplishment of the two
witnesses. If anyone in history ever had a good
name, it would be the two witnesses. They represent the fulfillment of two promised witnesses—
Moses and Elijah, crowning representatives of
the law and the prophets.

For 1,260 days, they have been witnesses for the
good name of God, and now their work is finished.
After being martyred, they are raised from the
dead and ascend to heaven in the sight of their
enemies. What a crowning achievement!

Revelation, Chapter 12

The ל *lamed* is a letter whose height is greater than all the other letters. Having a numerical value of thirty, it is flanked on one side of the *Aleph-beit* by the ך *kaf,* and on the other by the מ *mem.* The ך *kaf* is said to represent God's throne of glory; the מ *mem*, God's kingship. Together, the *mem, lamed,* and *kaf* form the Hebrew word, מלך *melek*, meaning "king."

Fascinating! Revelation 12 features the birth of the King:

> "And there appeared a great wonder in heaven; a woman clothed with the sun, and the moon under her feet, and upon her head a crown of twelve stars:
>
> "And she being with child cried, travailing in birth, and pained to be delivered.
>
> "And there appeared another wonder in heaven; and behold a great red dragon, having seven heads and ten horns, and seven crowns upon his heads.
>
> "And his tail drew the third part of the stars of heaven, and did cast them to the earth: and the dragon stood before the woman which was ready to be delivered, for to devour her child as soon as it was born.
>
> "And she brought forth a man child, who was to **rule** all nations with a rod of iron: and her child was caught up unto God, and to his throne" (Revelation 12:1-5).

Divine perfection is clearly shown in the miraculous birth of Jesus. Also, ל *lamed* is called:

"... the symbol of teaching and purpose ... That the tallest letter in the [*Aleph-beit*] is the one that implies *lamad*, teaching and learning, implies that this quality is man's highest endowment. Man's intellectual capacity is God's august gift, with which he can develop human consciousness of the Divine and transmit spirituality."[15]

It is appropriate then, that the twelfth chapter of Revelation is an abbreviated teaching, or didactic history, that tells the story of the woman, her man child, the dragon, the wilderness, Michael the Archangel, and the events of war in heaven and on earth. This story is a spiritual history that forms the core of the struggle between good and evil. It capsules the program of the King of kings.

The ל *lamed* is indeed "the symbol of teaching and purpose." Revelation 12, being a condensed teaching, corresponds perfectly with this twelfth letter of the Hebrew *Aleph-beit!*

Revelation, Chapter 13

The thirteenth letter, מ (ם) *mem*, signifies water. In its most ancient forms, it resembled waves of water. Its gematria is forty, the number associated in Scripture with testing or trial.

How fitting it is that this chapter features the beast who rises out of the *"sea"* to put Israel to the supreme test, ultimately to commit the *"abomination of desolation"* (Matt. 24:15), and sell out Israel after publicly agreeing to support them.

The letter מ *mem* is written in two forms: the open form of מ *mem* is used at the beginning or middle of a word, and the closed or "final form" of ם *mem* is used at the end of a word. For this reason, it is called "the symbol of the revealed and the concealed."[16]

The open form of מ *mem* is symbolic of that which is revealed and easily understood. On that note, it is interesting that Revelation deals with the beast out of the sea: *"... and all the world wondered after the beast"* (Rev. 13:3). The final development of the world system will be revealed to the entire world. On the other hand, the closed "final form" of ם *mem* speaks of that which is mysterious and not as easily discerned. Such is the future. No man can see into the future. It is closed to us. All we know is what we read in God's message through the prophets. We learn about the closed nature of prophetic truth by God's message to Daniel:

"... *shut up the words, and seal the book, even to the time of the end*" (Daniel 12:4).

We are also familiar with the strange passage in Revelation 10:4. The Lord told John,

"... *Seal up those things which the seven thunders uttered, and write them not*" (Revelation 10:4).

Such is the nature of the "final form" of ם *mem*. In fact, each of the five "final forms" in the Hebrew *Aleph-beit* have a prophetic significance.

Concerning Revelation 13, the open מ *mem* seems to refer to the first half of the chapter and the closed ם *mem* may refer to the second half. The chapter tells of two beasts who rise up from the sea and the earth. This number of the second beast appears concealed. The chapter ends with this cryptic statement:

"*Here is wisdom. Let him that **hath understanding** count the number of the beast: for it is the number of a man; and his number is Six hundred threescore and six*" (Rev. 13:18).

Revelation, Chapter 14

The letter **נ** (**ן**) *nun* has a numerical value of fifty. This letter is said to stand for "faithfulness, soul, and emergence." Like the letters **כ** (**ך**) *kaf* and **מ** (**ם**) *mem*, this fourteenth letter is written in two ways, the bent **נ** *nun* used at the beginning or in the midst of a word, and the straight **ן**

nun or "final form" used at the end of a word. The eleventh century Rabbi, Rashi, once wrote:

> "One who submits himself humbly to God's will, bending before Him like the bent [**נ**] nun, will stand straight and upright like the final [**ן**] nun when he eventually faces the Day of Judgment."[17]

The first five verses of Revelation 14 speak of the 144,000 on Mount Zion with the Lamb. They present the image of humble service, coupled with uprightness before the Lord. It perfectly suits the meaning of the letter **נ** (**ן**) *nun*.

This letter is also said to represent the soul, or *neshamah* in the Hebrew language, which is also called *ner,* or candle—reminding us of the middle lamp of the Menorah:

"Man is accountable for his thoughts, words and deeds, because God placed within his body a celestial light—his soul."[18]

The letter נ (ן) *nun* also stands for the quality of being perpetual and everlasting, and the blessing that comes from living a life of obedience. Again, we find a perfect match. Verse 9 says:

"Blessed are the dead which die in the Lord from henceforth: Yea saith the Spirit, that they may rest from their labors; and their works do follow them."

The letter is also said to reflect "downfall and simultaneous salvation ... נ *nun,* in itself, implies the outlook for hope, redemption and the eventual future resurrection: נ *nun* stands for *nephilah*, downfall, but implies at the same time the concepts of *ner* [candle] light in darkness and of *neshamah*, spirit in the body. No turmoil [bent נ *nun*] will last forever, because in the end it leads to the exalted ן *nun*."

Chapter 14 ends with a description of the harvest judgment—the terrible culmination of God's wrath. It is a dark time, out of which will flow the joy of the kingdom.

Revelation, Chapter 15

The ס *samech* has a nu-
merical value of sixty. In
shape, it is closed and
rounded. It is said to represent, "Divine support, both
in the active sense that God
provides support to man and
in the passive sense that
man relies on him." The

number sixty is said to depict completeness, in
the same way that ו *vav* and the number six speak
of the fullness of God's six days of creation.

The ס *samech* is also called the letter of the
"sign" [*siman*]. It speaks of the distinctive Divine
hallmarks that appear throughout Scripture. It is
therefore, significant that Revelation 15:1 begins:

> *"And I saw another **sign** in heaven, great and marvel-
> ous, seven angels having the seven last plagues; for in
> them is filled up the wrath of God."*

This is the sign of God's wrath. Of all the signs
in heaven, this is the one that men most fear. For
centuries they have joked that it would never
actually come. But their jokes were hollow; now it
is about to be unveiled. The saints sing the Song
of Moses, which we have studied at length in our
books HIDDEN PROPHECIES IN THE PSALMS
and HIDDEN PROPHECIES IN THE SONG OF

MOSES. This song of Moses is a prophecy about the final judgment of God which is about to begin.

The circular shape of ס *samech* is said to represent God as protector and the interior depicts Israel, who is dependent on His protection. As God's wrath is poured out, Israel will definitely need such protection.

"The center of the ס [*samech*] is an allusion to the [*Mishkan*], Tabernacle, the place where the Shekinah, God's Presence, dwelled during Israel's journey in the desert. The peripheral line of the ס [*samech*] represents the camps of Israel, which surrounded the sanctuary.

"The same was the case when Israel settled in the Holy Land. The center of the ס [*samech*] depicts the *beit hamikdash*, Holy Temple, the abode of Divine Presence."[19]

In yet another amazing correspondence Revelation 15:5 and 8 says:

"*After that I looked, and, behold, the **temple** of the tabernacle of the testimony in heaven was opened.*"
"*And the temple was filled with smoke from the glory of God, and from his power...*"

It is remarkable to see that the very heart of this letter's meaning beams through the eight verses of this chapter. This is the significant place in Scripture where we see the opening of the Temple in heaven.

Revelation, Chapter 16

The ע *ayin* has a numerical value of seventy. This number is said to be "critical in the turning points of history."

E. W. Bullinger points out that as the product of seven and ten, it "signifies perfect spiritual order carried out with all spiritual power and significance."[20] This chapter reflects precisely that message, as the seven vials of God's wrath are poured out upon an unrepentant world. Indeed, this chapter marks the great turning point of history, as the corrupt world system finally dies, to be replaced by the era of Messianic rule.

The ע *ayin* is also said to be the letter of "sight and insight,"[21] since the name *ayin* means "eye." The eye—the organ of vision and direction—is spoken of as bringing the entire universe into focus. The judgments of this chapter are a focal point of human history: the eye of God is now focused in wrath.

The letter ע *ayin* is also taught as representative of "the tempted eye" of mankind. Just as the eye can lead one into purity and spiritual insight, so it can turn to lust and evil influence.

With the pouring out of the first vial of wrath, we find in verse 2:

"... there fell a noisome and grievous sore upon the men which had the mark of the beast, and upon them which worshipped his image."

With the eye, men had paid homage to the image of the beast. Now, they are about to pay in full, under the discerning eye of God. This symbol of God's eye may also be viewed in the context of a mystery that began in ages past at the tower of Babel. John writes:

"... and great Babylon came in remembrance before God, to give unto her the cup of the wine of the fierceness of his wrath" (Revelation 16:19).

One modern symbol for the tower of Babel shows an unfinished pyramid with an "all seeing eye" suspended above it. Genesis 11:5 puts this theme in its proper perspective:

"And the LORD came down to see the city and the tower, which the children of men builded" (Genesis 11:5).

The ע *ayin* appears to be quite appropriate for this chapter as the final judgment of God commences upon an unbelieving human race.

Revelation, Chapter 17

"The **פ** (**ף**) *peh* stands for the mouth, the organ of speech."[22] So begins the commentary on this letter, which has a numerical value of 80. And, in like manner, chapter 17 begins with a speech:

"And there came one of the seven angels which had the seven vials, and talked with me, saying unto me Come hither; I will shew unto thee the judgment of the great whore that sitteth upon many waters."

And so begins a proclamation of the destruction of Mystery Babylon the Great. The placing of this story under the **פ** (**ף**) *peh* alludes back to the meaning of the name Babylon—babbling. Also, this chapter features a speech, during which an angel expounds to John the details of the evil woman's destruction. As the angel speaks, John listens in stunned silence. This is remarkably like the Jewish teaching that **פ** (**ף**) *peh* has both a bent form **פ** (used at the beginning or in the midst of a word) which symbolically alludes to a closed mouth, and a long open form **ף** (used at the end of a word) which alludes to an open mouth. The rabbis say that "just as the mouth should sometimes be open and sometimes be closed," so there is a time to speak and a time to remain silent. At this time, while John listens, the message is spoken by the angel with great clarity: Mystery Babylon is about to be destroyed. Rabbi Munk writes:

> "The power of intelligent speech gives man the highest rank among the categories of existence.... Through speech, man can articulate the soul's insights and concepts, and communicate them to others; their intelligent speech is the basis of all humanity and civilization."[23]

In Revelation 17, we find the ultimate conclusion to "humanity and civilization"—Mystery Babylon. The term Babylon or Babel refers to the powers of speech. This mystery, which is about to fall under the final judgment of God takes us back to the tower of Babel, when all men spoke only one language. Their communication skills were used to plot against God. During the construction of their ultimate idolatry, God confounded their powers of speech and added 70 languages to the human race! Here, God's final judgment commences. What started at Babel is thus concluded.

It is most fitting that the story of the "speech" concludes in this remarkable chapter which corresponds to פ (ף) *peh*, the symbol of speech and silence!

Revelation, Chapter 18

Revelation 18 completes the destruction of the world system of Babylon. The kings of the earth express great lamentation over her fall. But there is quite a different picture in heaven, as seen in Revelation 18:20:

"Rejoice over her, thou heaven, and ye holy apostles and prophets; for God hath avenged you on her."

A righteous God has acted in judgment, and it is time for rejoicing in heaven. It seems significant then, that **צ** *tzaddi* is the letter associated with righteousness. This is probably because **צ** *tzaddi* is quite close to the Hebrew word, *tzaddik*, which means "righteousness."[24]

This letter, having a numerical value of 90, is said to depict "the righteousness of God and devout human beings." *Tzaddi* also has two forms: a bent **צ** form and a straightened **ץ** form that appears at the end of a word.

These two forms are said to be a picture of righteous man. The bent form pictures his humility in this world. The straightened form shows that he will stand tall and erect in the world to come. The last verse of this chapter is a clear reference to the righteous, which God has avenged:

> *"And in her was found the blood of prophets, and of saints, and of all that were slain upon the earth"* (Rev. 18:24).

It is also appropriate that the **צ** *tzaddi*, which stands for righteousness, should correspond with the message of this chapter—the judgment of Mystery Babylon. The saints in heaven make it quite clear in the following verse:

> *"For true and **righteous are his judgments**: for he hath judged the great whore, which did corrupt the earth with her fornication, and hath avenged the blood of his servants at her hand"* (Revelation 19:2).

This final judgment of God upon a wicked humanity is shown to be an outgrowth of His righteousness.

Revelation, Chapter 19

The ק *koph* is the symbol of "holiness and growth cycles."[25] It "alludes to God's *kedushah*, holiness." Its gematria is 100.

Revelation 19:1-2 says:

> *"And after these things I heard a great voice of much people in heaven, saying Alleluia: Salvation and glory, and honor, and power, unto the Lord our God:*
>
> *"For true and righteous are his judgments: for he hath judged the great whore, which did corrupt the earth with her fornication, and hath avenged the blood of his servants at her hand."*

This chapter opens with a "Hallelujah Chorus" in verses 1-6. In verses 7-10, we find the marriage supper of the Lamb. Then, in verses 11-21, we see the Second Coming of the *"King of kings and Lord of lords,"* and the destruction of the beast and those who follow him.

At last, the Messiah has stepped out of heaven. He arrives on earth to establish the Kingdom.

The ק *Koph* is also said to represent *hakafah*, the cycle of growth. Regarding ק *koph,* Rabbi Munk writes:

"The cycle of human history began in *Gan Eden* [the Garden of Eden], where man's recognition of God was as clear as day and where man and all animals lived together in perfect harmony. Though mankind's awareness of *Hashem* [God] weakened in course of history, it will return to its starting point in Messianic times..."[26]

"Messianic times" begins in this very chapter!

Another amazing insight concerning ק *koph* is that its spelling is the Hebrew word for monkey:

"The fact that the same letter koph represents both *kedushah* and an animal that is a parody of humanity offers a deep insight about man's role. Man is created in the image of God and is only a little lower than the angels (Ps. 8:6). Though he can never attain God's holiness, he is charged with emulating Him and is assured that he can scale celestial heights. But he can do so only if his efforts are concerted and sincere. If man acts as an 'image of God,' his potential is boundless. If he is merely a poor imitation of what man should be, he is hardly better than a primate."[27]

This is an extremely pertinent comment, in view of the fact that the beast and his followers are thrown into the lake of fire at the conclusion of this chapter. The beast was created as a man who might have pursued the holiness of God. Instead, he became like an animal and was destroyed.

Revelation, Chapter 20

Because of its association with the Hebrew word *rashah,* "wickedness," ר *resh* stands for the wicked.[28] In like manner, this chapter deals with the binding of the old master of wickedness himself—Satan—for a thousand years, and his release and rebellion at the end of that time:

> "And I saw an angel come down from heaven, having the key of the bottomless pit and a great chain in his hand.
>
> "And he laid hold on the dragon, that old serpent, which is the Devil, and Satan, and bound him a thousand years.
>
> "And cast him into the bottomless pit, and shut him up, and set a seal upon him, that he should deceive the nations no more, till the thousand years should be fulfilled: and after that he must be loosed a little season" (Revelation 20:1-3).

Its numerical value is 200 and is a multiple of two, the number of division, duality and conflict. Likewise, this chapter tells about a final conflict led by the devil after he is released.

This chapter also deals with the judgment of the Great White Throne, in which the wicked of all time will be judged and thrown into a lake of fire:

"And I saw a great white throne, and him that sat on it, from whose face the earth and the heaven fled away; and there was found no place for them.

"And I saw the dead, small and great, stand before God; and the books were opened: and another book was opened, which is the book of life: and the dead were judged out of those things which were written in the books, according to their works.

"And the sea gave up the dead which were in it; and death and hell delivered up the dead which were in them: and they were judged every man according to their works.

"And death and hell were cast into the lake of fire. This is the second death.

"And whosoever was not found written in the book of life was cast into the lake of fire" (Revelation 20:11-15).

What more needs to be said? This chapter in its entirety deals with the subject of wickedness as portrayed in the ר *Resh*. Surely, we must marvel at the way in which the Hebrew *Aleph-beit* corresponds to the 22 chapters of Revelation. The divine design of the book is irrefutable!

Revelation, Chapter 21

The commentary on ש *shin* opens with the following words: "The ש *shin* stands high among the Sacred Letters because it represents two names of God: *Shaddai*, the All-Sufficient, Unlimited One, and *Shalom*, Peace."[29] Its numerical value is 300, a multiple of 3, which to Christians, stands for the person and character of God.

The ש *shin* is engraved on the Mezuza—a small container of Scripture found on the doors of every Jewish home, representing God's protection for those who live there. It is appropriate, therefore, that this chapter is devoted to the arrival of the New Jerusalem—our eternal home.

Furthermore, the city has twelve gates engraved with the names of the twelve tribes of Israel. Perhaps they are engraved on heavenly Mezuzas! Since the ש *shin* corresponds to this chapter, one might speculate that those twelve gates each have a Mezuza! Why not? After all, this is the city of *Shaddai*!

Revelation 21:27 may also be a reference to a heavenly Mezuza:

*"And there shall in no wise enter into it anything that defileth, neither whatsoever worketh abomination, or maketh a lie: but **they which are written in the Lamb's book of life**"* (Rev. 21:27).

It is remarkable that such a "book" of life is also mentioned in Daniel (12:1). We have noted that the ש *shin* also corresponds with the theme of Daniel (see page 227).

Finally, this is the city of God's peace. According to Rabbi Munk, the ש *shin* stands for *shalom*, meaning "peace." No better analogy could be made than to recognize that the very name, Jerusalem, means "city of peace."

The rabbis teach that ש *shin* also stands for *sheker* (falsehood and corruption) or that which is rejected by God. Verse 27 of this chapter is a testimony to exactly that rejection. No falsehood or corruption will be allowed in the holy city. *Shaddai* (as typified by the ש *shin*) is seen protecting the inhabitants from those who would defile, or work an abomination, or make a lie.

Revelation, Chapter 22

The ת *tahv* symbolizes the Hebrew word, *emet,* "truth." In Hebrew, this word is said to be an acrostic that stands for "God is the Eternal King, in the infinite past, present and future."[30] In this chapter, verse 6 verifies this reading:

"And he said unto me, These sayings are faithful and ***true****: and the Lord God of the holy prophets sent his angel to shew unto his servants the things which must shortly be done."*

Also, truth is epitomized in Jesus, who said,

"I am the way, the ***truth****, and the life ..."* (John. 14:6).

This letter has a numerical value of 400, a multiple of 4 and 40, the numbers associated with the material creation and the testing of man. Rabbinic teaching says that ת *tahv* represents "man's final destination." It is also said to typify divine perfection—the very subject of this chapter:

"I am Alpha and Omega, the beginning and the end, the first and the last" (verse 13).

We are now brought full circle back to where we started in Revelation. Jesus, the *"Word,"* announces Himself as the first and last letters of the Alphabet. The final book of the Bible is the "Revelation of Jesus Christ." Its twenty-two chapters speak of His character and His work. And now we know that even the letters of the Hebrew *Aleph-beit* expound His truth:

> *"And, behold, I come quickly; and my reward is with me, to give every man according as his work shall be.*
> *"I am Alpha and Omega, the beginning and the end, the first and the last"* (Rev. 22:12-13).

One day in the not-too-distant future, the Church will depart this earth. When it does, the sealing of national Israel's righteous remnant (144,000) will mark a new appointment in human history. As Jews, they will have a deep understanding of the symbolism which we have reviewed. They will recognize that Revelation is a Jewish book. It will seem that its words were written for them ... even directly to them. This will stand as a sign to the Jew that the entire Bible—not just the Old Testament—is divinely inspired.

For the first time, the Lord is allowing us to see these beautiful patterns. This can only mean that we must be drawing very close to the events that will bring forth the Tribulation.

Chapter Five Notes:

1. Rabbi Michael L. Munk, THE WISDOM IN THE HEBREW ALPHABET (Brooklyn, N. Y., Mesorah), p. 19.

2. Ibid., p. 18.

3. Ibid., p. 43.

4. Ibid., p. 71.

5. Ibid., p. 78.

6. Ibid., p. 90.

7. Ibid., p. 94.

8. E. W. Bullinger, NUMBER IN SCRIPTURE (Grand Rapids, Kregel) p. 150.

9. Munk, WISDOM, p. 105.

10. Ibid., p. 112.

11. Ibid., p. 119.

12. Ibid., p. 125.

13. Ibid., p. 128.

14. Ibid., p. 133.

15. Ibid., pp. 138-139.

16. Ibid., p. 143.

17. Ibid., p. 152.

18. Ibid., p. 153.

19. Ibid., p. 160.

20. Bullinger, NUMBER, p. 270.

21. Munk, p. 171.

22. Ibid., p. 180.

23. Ibid.

24. Ibid., p. 189.

25. Ibid., p. 194.

26. Ibid., p. 197.

27. Ibid., p. 198.

28. Ibid., p. 199.

29. Ibid., p. 207.

30. Ibid., p. 218.

Chapter Six

The Ancient Design of the Old Testament

Our study of Revelation led us to continue an examination of the of the relationship between the ancient Hebrew *Aleph-beit* and the structure of Scripture. With the knowledge that the Jews once considered the Old Testament to have an arrangement of 22 books, that was the next natural place for us to begin a search.

Once again, we were amazed to discover the same large-scale symbolic correlation. Though we're looking at a different area of the Bible, many of the same ideas from THE WISDOM OF THE HEBREW ALPHABET will be applied here in much the same way they were in the preceding chapter.

Roughly, since the time of the Reformation,

Christian scholars have held to the Old Testament canon or formal structure of 39 books—Genesis through Malachi. Before that time, various arrangements of the sacred writings were favored.

For example, Augustine (354-430) declared the Old Testament to consist of 44 books. But his compilation included books that were later considered "apocryphal," or lacking in divine inspiration in their original autographs.

It has been pointed out that his 44 books were exactly twice the number of books considered to be the correct number by theologians and commentators in the first century. At that time, as well as later, in the second and third centuries, the Old Testament was considered to have 22 books.

Of all the early church fathers, Origin (185-254) was considered to be one of the greatest Christian biblical scholars. Origin's statement concerning the books of the Old Testament, as preserved by Eusebius, reads as follows:

> "We should not be ignorant that there are twenty-two books of the [Old] Testament, according to the tradition of the Hebrews, corresponding to the number of letters in their alphabet ... These are the twenty-two books according to the Hebrew: ..."[1]

In a commentary on the Psalms, Origin expands

upon the idea that the books of the Old Testament are intimately connected with the wisdom of the Hebrew alphabet:

> "For as the twenty-two letters appear to form an introduction to the wisdom and the divine teachings which are written down for man and woman in these characters, so the twenty-two divinely-inspired books form an ABC into the wisdom of God and an introduction to the knowledge of all that is."[2]

Note that Origin's training brought him to believe in the Bible as an abecedary (see page 117) that ranged from א *aleph* through ת *tahv*. In other words, he thought of the Old Testament as a large-scale structure, inexorably linked to the wisdom traditionally taught in the Hebrew *Alephbeit*. This is precisely the message that was impressed upon us during the preceding study in Revelation. Strangely, the alphabetic structure of the Bible is a concept that has slipped into obscurity over the years.

Likewise, the noted Jewish historian Flavius Josephus, writing in the last decade of the first century, points out that the Jewish Bible of his day (we think of it as the Old Testament) had just 22 books. In his treatise "Against Apion," he writes:

> "For we have not an innumerable multitude of books among us, disagreeing from and contradicting one another [as the Greeks have], but only twenty-two

The Hebrew *Aleph-beit*

א   **Aleph** letter for God as "Creator and King."

ב   **Beit** letter for "house and Temple."

ג   **Gimel** letter for " loving kindness and culmination."

ד   **Dalet** letter for "the door."

ה   **Hay** letter for the "breath of God."

ו   **Vav** letter for "completion and redemption."

ז   **Zayin** "focal point of sustenance and struggle."

ח   **Chet** letter for "transcendence, life, and grace."

ט   **Tet** letter for "serpent and objective good."

י   **Yod** letter for "creation and metaphysical."

כ ך   **Kaf** letter for "crowning accomplishment."

ל   **Lamed** letter for "teaching and learning."

מ ם   **Mem** letter for "water," "revealed, and concealed."

נ ן   **Nun** letter for "faithfulness, soul, and emergence."

ס   **Samech** letter for "support and Divine presence."

ע   **Ayin** letter for "sight and insight."

פ ף   **Peh** letter for "mouth and speech."

צ ץ   **Tzaddi** letter for "righteousness and humility."

ק   **Koph** letter for "holiness and growth cycles."

ר   **Resh** letter for "the wicked."

ש   **Shin** letter for "Divine power and provision."

ת   **Tav** letter for "truth and perfection."

Five letters have two forms—the first form is used if the letter appears at the beginning or in the midst of a word. The final form is used if the letter appears at the end of a word. The five final forms are:

ך Kaf, ם Mem, ן Nun, ף Peh, and ץ Tzaddi.

books, which contain the records of all the past times; which are justly believed to be divine; and of them, five belong to Moses, which contain his laws and the traditions of the origin of mankind till his death. This interval of time was little short of three thousand years; but as to the time from the death of Moses till the reign of Artaxerxes king of Persia, who reigned after Xerxes, the prophets, who were after Moses wrote down what was done in their times in thirteen books. The remaining four books contain hymns to God, and precepts for the conduct of human life."[3]

It is clear that the canon of the Old Testament in the days of Jesus was understood to correspond to the structure of the Hebrew *Aleph-beit*. As we shall see, the basic organization of the Old Testament's original 22 books has survived intact and in order even to our very day. And their metaphoric meanings are still reflected in the wisdom of the Hebrew *Aleph-beit*!

The Early Writings

As we begin to look at this organized arrangement, we should point out at the beginning that we will be following the order of Old Testament Scripture as it appears in today's canon of 39 books. To arrive at a total number of 22 books, all that is necessary is to combine certain books, as was the custom in the early Jewish scrolls.

For example, Judges and Ruth were once a single writing. I & II Samuel were combined, as were I & II Kings and I & II Chronicles. Ezra and

Nehemiah were originally joined together under the title, "I & II Ezra." Also, Jeremiah and Lamentations were a single book. Finally, the twelve Minor Prophets were originally united in a single document.

When the books of the Old Testament *in their present order* are simply recombined in the above manner, the result is an arrangement of 22 books. We shall examine this grouping in the same way we looked at the 22 chapters of Revelation. Amazingly, as we move from א *aleph* through ת *tahv*—from Genesis through Malachi—we discover that the meanings of the *Aleph-beit* display the same remarkable correspondence to the Old Testament as they do to the book of Revelation.

Genesis *(Aleph)*

Genesis, the book of beginnings, is the ultimate statement of God's power and sovereignty. Here, He is expounded as Creator, Sovereign, Sustainer and Redeemer, who creates a perfect environment for man and woman—the primary purpose  of His creation. He is the one and only constant throughout the events of their fall and the promise of mankind's redemption.

Through their sin and the sins of their progeny, He develops a redemptive plan that stretches out across the ages. Genesis is the setting for this immense journey. Without the simple understanding of man's creation and fall, the rest of the Bible becomes an inexplicable chronicle of man's repeated failure. The contrast between man's sinful nature and God's sinless perfection forms the foundation of divinely-inspired Scripture.

The א *aleph*, the first letter of the Hebrew *Aleph-beit*, represents the number one. Remember that THE WISDOM OF THE HEBREW ALPHABET portrays א *aleph* as symbolizing the "One and Only, the Eternal, the Omnipotent God."[4] It is said to be the master letter, proclaiming both the name of God and His divinity. It is the link between heaven and earth; between God and the finite, physical creation.

The Bible's first sentence states this theme with great force:

"In the beginning, God created the heaven and the earth."

Here, the Sovereign God of the universe steps forth to create everything that we are able to perceive today. He is the source and the end of everything.

As we pointed out in an earlier chapter, this first sentence has as its centerpiece the א *aleph* and the ת *tahv* (see pages 29 and 115). Thus, the end of creation is stated from the very beginning, as when Jesus proclaims in Revelation 1:8:

"I am Alpha and Omega, the beginning and the ending, saith the Lord, which is , and which was, and which is to come, the Almighty."

The over-arching theme of Genesis is God, His creation, His judgments in the flood and at Babel, and His redemptive covenant with fallen man. As the first book of the Bible concludes, we observe God's grace through the history of the Patriarchs—Abraham, Isaac, and Jacob.

Truly, the oneness of God in person and purpose is the predominant feature of Genesis, and א *aleph*, the number one, is the perfect character to represent this theme.

Exodus *(Beit)*

The ב *beit* represents the number two. It is said to be the number of blessing and creation—of beginning. *Baruch*, the Hebrew word for blessing begins with ב *beit*. The first two Hebrew words of Genesis 1:1 also begin with this letter (***Bereshit***  ***barah***). They are translated into English as, *"In the beginning ... created ..."*

The ב *beit* is also said to be the letter of duality; good versus evil and right versus wrong. It describes the curse of disobedience that accompanies the blessing of obedience. Many Christian expositors have also taught that two is the number of division, opposition, or enmity.

Most significantly of all, Jews declare ב *beit* to be the letter that represents the house, the home, the house of meeting or the Holy Temple, since the very pronunciation of this letter forms the Hebrew word that means "house."

On the basis of this analysis, it is amazing to observe that the driving force of Exodus is the conflict between good and evil, seen in the house of Pharaoh versus the house of God. The hardened heart of Pharaoh is pitted against the Chosen People and the goodness of God, who raises up a deliverer for them in the person of Moses. The

second half of Exodus centers around God's revelation to those people at Sinai, and the building
of His House—the Tabernacle.

The 40 chapters of Exodus are divided at the
center of the book. The first 20 chapters deal with
Israel's redemption from Egypt, preservation in
the wilderness and the giving of the Ten Commandments. The last 20 chapters deal with the
revelation of the Mosaic Covenant and the people's
response to it. In these chapters, the theme of
good versus evil is once again played out, as Israel
willfully breaks the covenant and Moses personally intercedes for Israel's salvation.

Most important of all, God establishes His presence among the people by giving them the *Mishkan*—the Holy Tabernacle, which can quite cor-
rectly be called God's "**house**," since the mercy
seat atop the Ark of the Covenant acted as the
location for His presence. At the conclusion of
Exodus, Moses inspects the finished Tabernacle
and pronounces his blessing upon it. Thus, the
house is established.

Perfectly matching the declared meaning of ב
beit, Exodus not only features the establishment
of a house, but a blessing for obedience and a curse
for disobedience. Chapter 40 pictures the incred-
ibly beautiful scene in which God fills the completed Tabernacle with His glory. The house is
complete.

Leviticus *(Gimel)*

The ג *gimel*, third letter of the He-
brew alphabet, is also used as the
number three. It is said to be "the
symbol of kindness and culmination."
The ג *gimel* "is cognate to *gamol*,
which means to **nourish** until completely ripe."⁵ Christian expositors
have often noted that the number 3 denotes the
Godhead and, by implication, **completeness** or
fullness.

The book of Leviticus is said to represent Israel's
progress from Egyptian redemption to the walk of
service as a kingdom of priests and a nation of
holiness. In its first 17 chapters, it lays out the
laws concerning offerings, priestly consecration
and national atonement. Chapters 18 through 27
deal with the sanctified walk with God.

Israel is urged to walk the walk of holiness with
God; to be sanctified through the laws that bring
continued fellowship with God. Such holiness
required the Israelites to be set apart from the
Gentile civilizations around them and being separated unto God. In return, God provided for their
physical and spiritual nourishment.

The ג *gimel* is said to represent God's loving-
kindness and goodness. In response to these qualities, the spiritual man must attempt to reflect

them in his life. It is interesting that Leviticus is devoted to **nourishing** and perfecting of this sort of man. In obedience to the law, the defilement that separates man from God is removed, providing the way for the walk of fellowship. Leviticus 1:1 begins:

> *"And the Lord called unto Moses, and spake unto him out of the tabernacle of the congregation ..."*

Having established His presence among His people, He graciously acts to provide for them a way of fellowship. But the idea of culmination or completion is also a major theme of Leviticus.

Someone once said that it took God only one night to take Israel out of Egypt. However, it took 40 years to take Egypt out of Israel. In Exodus, the Jews are redeemed and set up in holiness as a kingdom of priests. In Leviticus, they are taught how to walk with God in fellowship, in order to fulfill the priestly call.

This is Israel's calling. As a matter of fact, the Hebrew title of this book is *Vayikra*, meaning, "and He called." As we have noted, the book opens with God calling to Moses, giving a message to the people concerning the sacrifices and offerings they are to make.

Leviticus also features major redemptive themes: the Five Offerings, the ministry of the High Priest, and the Seven Feasts of Israel. In all of these, the culmination of the redemptive pattern is quite apparent. In them, the figure of Christ's finished work is literally projected toward the Kingdom Age.

The offerings picture His submission to His Father's will; His sinless service; His close relationship with the faithful; His role as burden-bearer of our guilt; and His payment for sin. Aaron, the High Priest, is a type of Christ, our eternal High Priest. Israel's Seven Feasts are a prophetic overview that culminates in His Second Coming. He is the very picture of loving-kindness, combined with the power to bring the affairs of this world to culmination.

The real theme of the book is encapsulated in chapter 19, verse 2:

"Speak unto all the congregation of the children of Israel, and say unto them, Ye shall be holy: for I the Lord your God am holy."

God shows the people the way to walk with Him in fellowship. Though He required certain standards for fellowship, the holiness required of the people is clearly delineated. The people will never be in doubt about what God requires. In the Law, He gives them what they need to seek His holiness—and completion.

Numbers *(Dalet)*

The ד *dalet* is the number four. It is cognate with the Hebrew, דלת *delet*, "door." "The ד *dalet* also alludes to דל *dahl* (pauper), who knocks on doors begging for alms ... The shape of the ד *dalet* is like that of a door with its lintel spreading right and left and its doorpost reaching up and down."

With this rabbinic teaching in view, it is interesting to observe that the book of Numbers could well be entitled "Israel at the Door." The subject of the book is Israel's wilderness march. In fact, Jews refer to this book as *Bemidbar*, meaning, "in the wilderness."

Numbers covers a time period of a little less than 40 years. During this time, the people wander in the wilderness. Their goal is **entrance** into the Promised Land.

Having given them the directions for fellowship in Leviticus, God now puts them through the divine discipline that will bring them to spiritual maturity.

The first 10 chapters detail the preparation of Israel to enter the Promised Land. Chapters 10 through approximately 25 show how the Israelites fail to enter that land. As they march through the wilderness, they rebel at Kadesh. A bit later, Korah rebels against Moses and Aaron. The **door** of entry into the land is closed as a result of Israel's own rebellion.

Chapters 26-36 finally show an Israel ready to enter the land after 40 years of wandering. Once again, the **door** of entry is opened. These chapters detail the offerings that God will require, the details of tribal inheritance and a final review of the social codes that will regulate the lives of the Jews when they enter the land.

As they camp in the plains of Moab across the Jordan from Jericho, the new generation is preparing to enter the land. They are at the brink of inheriting the land.

The number four, ד *dalet,* represents the material creation with its four divisions of the day, four seasons, four tides, four cardinal directions, and four phases of the moon, as well as the attributes of God's creativity.

In Genesis 10:5, men were divided according to four designations: *"... lands ... tongues ... families ... nations."* Thus, four has been called the number of the Kingdom. Both meanings of ד *dalet* are in view at the end of the book. Israel is poised to enter the land of the kingdom. It is as if they stand once again before an open **door**.

Deuteronomy *(Hay)*

To the Jews, this letter, with its numerical value of five, is also symbolic of the divine name of God and His creation. In Hebrew writings, the letter ה *hay* is used as an abbreviation for the Name of God. As such, it invokes interpretations of His creative power, grace, and redemptive promise.

This letter is also associated with repentance and mercy. The Hebrew word *teshuvah*, meaning "repentance," can be separated into two parts: *teshuv*, followed by the letter ה *hay*. Using this analysis, the rabbis say the word becomes "return to God." As we have already done in the discussion of Revelation, we refer once again to a quote from Rabbi Munk, as he writes:

"The Passover Haggadah [story] speaks of two new songs of rejoicing, one in the feminine form [shirah chadashah] and one in the masculine [shir chadash]. We introduce Hallel, the psalms of praise for the Exodus, by calling it shirah chadashah, a new song, spelled with the feminine suffix ה hay. The song of Messianic Day, however, is described as shir chadash, in the masculine form. Before Hallel, when we are about to thank God for redeeming us from the Egyptian bondage, we use the feminine form to suggest that the redemption was incomplete, as it was followed by other exiles and sufferings, each more painful than the preceding one. This as yet unended chain of national suffering is similar to labor pangs which ease up for a short period only to be followed by more severe pain. Indeed, the tribulations of Israel are called the birth-pangs of the Messiah."[6]

This commentary on ה *hay* bears a startling similarity to the culmination of the Torah that is found at the conclusion of Deuteronomy. It is the "Song of Moses," found in the 32nd chapter. Moses' song addresses the central subject of Israel's tribulation. In fact, if there is any song that should remind Israel of the redemption from Egyptian bondage, it is the Song of Moses.

This is the song of Israel's redemption from seemingly overwhelming enemy forces. In it, Jehovah is called the *"Rock of his* [Israel's] *salvation"* (Deuteronomy 32:15). But the song also tells the sad tale of Israel's infidelity.

"Of the Rock that begat thee thou art unmindful, and hast forgotten God that formed thee" (v. 18).

The overall pattern of Moses' song prophesies Israel's apostasy, followed by God's judgment of His people and their ultimate return to Him. Its main theme is the Lord's deliverance of His people—first from Egypt, then in the far future during the judgments of the Tribulation.

"Rejoice, O ye nations, with his people: for he will avenge the blood of his servants, and will render vengeance to his adversaries, and will be merciful unto his land, and to his people" (v. 43).

Overall, Deuteronomy is a detailed account of Israel's final תשובה *teshuvah* (return to God). It begins with God's review of His great accomplishments for His people. Then, it fully expounds the Law, informing the people about that which God expects of them. Finally, along with the prophecies of Israel's apostasy, God's future covenant promise is clearly stated. All this is in remarkable conformity with the stated meaning of ה *hay*.

Among Christians, five is known as the number of grace. Through His grace, the Lord will complete His plan, regardless of man's insufficiency.

Joshua *(Vav)*

The ‫ו‬ *vav*, the sixth letter of the alphabet, has a gematria (numerical value) of six. According to rabbinic commentary, it denotes physical completion:

"The physical world was completed in six days and a complete self-contained object consists of six dimensions: above and below, right and left, before and behind ... The Jewish nation, too, is complete, self-contained, unique; that is why the number six is so prominent in the story of its growth to nationhood."[7]

The story of Joshua, son of Nun, is the story of a man who was born a slave in Egypt, but who entered the Promised Land as a conqueror. Not only did he conquer Canaan, but he also participated in the settlement of the Land and stated the conditions that God would require for continued settlement. Thus, the entire book of Joshua is given to entering, conquering, and occupying the Land.

It is appropriate then, that ‫ו‬ *vav* is called the letter of "completion, redemption, and transformation." Joshua is a type of Christ, our Redeemer, who completes, redeems, and transforms those who follow Him. The *"captain of the host of the Lord"* (Joshua 5:14) is thought by most Christians to be an appearance of the pre-incarnate Christ.

To quote Rabbi Munk again:

> "The letter ו vav is the prefix of conjunction; it unites manifold, even opposing concepts. It is the link connecting heaven and earth. Its form is that of a hook, as indeed its name וו [vav] means 'hook.' The vav links words and phrases to form sentences; it joins sentences into paragraphs and chapters; it connects one chapter to another; and even unites books. It may also be translated in the English word, 'and'."[8]

The events of the book of Joshua take place over a period of approximately 15 years. Taken as a whole, they form a kind of a connection or conjunction between Israel's wilderness march and the final disposition of tribal lands. Put another way, Joshua provides a transitional connection between the wanderings of Exodus, Leviticus, Numbers, and Deuteronomy and the administered Land under the Judges.

But the redemption didn't come without anguish. An important Hebrew word of conjunction is ויהי vayehi, meaning, "and it happened" or, "and it came to pass," as in Joshua 4:1. This word begins with a ו vav. When it appears in the text, it connects one key element of the narrative to the next.

But ויהי vayehi acts as more than a mere conjunction. It also has the meaning of "pain, anguish, or grief." It is said to indicate that where there is God's redemptive action, there is also anguish. The conquest of Canaan didn't come without failures such as Ai and the deception of the Gibeonites. In Joshua 24:29, we see the final use of the word והיה *vayehi.*

> *"And it came to pass after these things, that Joshua the son of Nun, the servant of the Lord, died, being an hundred and ten years old"* (Joshua 24:29).

This is a transition to the book of Judges, which stands in stark contrast to the faithful, conquering, obedient people under Joshua. At this point, Israel truly enters a new era.

Judges, Ruth *(Zayin)*

We have combined these two books into one, just as they were in Israel's ancient scrolls. Their basic meaning is characterized by the Hebrew letter ז *zayin*. The numerical value of this letter is seven. Rabbi Munk writes:

"As such, it denotes the spiritual values that were the purpose of Creation. God created the universe in six days and rested on the seventh ..."[9]

The ז *zayin* is said to be the letter of "spirit, sustenance, and struggle."

Judges and Ruth are set in a period of Israel's history that especially focuses on the contrast between faithfulness and faithlessness. Under Joshua, the people hit a high water mark of faith. They obtained God's promises because of their desire to cleave to the role model set by Joshua. But toward the end of his life, Joshua had warned them that they must choose whom they would serve—either God or idols. Spiritual degeneration ensued. By the time of Judges, *"every man did that which was right in his own eyes"* (Judges 21:25).

It is in this setting that the meaning of ז *zayin* becomes interesting. It is said to represent the "focal point," or center of peace. Rabbis point out that "seven comprises the six physical directions of expansion (east, west, north, south, up, down) plus one, representing its own individual focal point." The commentary continues:

> "Figuratively, [the human] condition is likened to the six directions—east, south, west, north, up and down—that surround every human being wherever he is. The directions are the influences that work on him incessantly. They are outside of man, at a distance from his essence, but he is never free of them, always surrounded by them. The seventh factor is the placid center of it all—the inner man who is the object of all the forces, but is not a part of them. How well he succeeds in shaping and maintaining his identity in accordance with the spiritual dictates of his soul is the challenge and purpose of life."[10]

This quote is applicable to Israel's Judges, particularly because each of them operated under conditions ranging from spiritual apathy to open hostility, both from internal and external enemies. The Hebrew title of the Judges was *"Shophetim."* This word carries the meaning of "ruler, deliverer, or savior." The Judges were not only called upon to maintain a system of justice, but to liberate and deliver the people. This is the very theme of ז *zayin*.

Additionally, the name זין *zayin* is the Hebrew word for "weapon." It is commonly seen as a symbol of self-defense under trying conditions. Many of the judges were great warriors who delivered the Israelites from oppressive enemies.

Such deliverance was necessary from time to time because the people had a continuing tendency to adopt the pagan practices of surrounding nations. Having forgotten God, they found themselves impoverished and imperiled. Thus, the theme of Judges is that of struggle, punctuated by spiritual intervention, in order that the people might be sustained. The Judges, themselves, provided the "placid center" in the midst of this struggle.

Spiritual strength in the midst of tribulation is also the beautiful narrative theme of Ruth. She provides a picture of faith in a world beset by famine, sickness, and death.

Ruth was a woman of Moab who, following the death of her husband, agreed to accept the people and faith of her Judean mother-in-law, Naomi. She found redemption in Boaz—a near kinsman—who became her husband. Thus, her steadfastness was rewarded as she was accepted into the lineage of Judah which became the house of David. During all her adventures, she lived with a calm inner strength that was independent of the turmoil in which she found herself.

Rabbi Munk further notes that the Hebrew word זן *zahn*, beginning with the letter ז *zayin*, is the verb, "to sustain." As such, this letter "conveys to man that the Omnipotent One will assure him success in his necessary endeavors for physical survival."[11] Judges and Ruth both carry this theme to perfection.

I & II Samuel *(Chet)*

About the letter ח *chet*, Rabbi Munk writes, "Going beyond seven, the number eight symbolizes man's ability to transcend the limitations of physical existence. Thus, with a gematria, or numerical value of eight, ח *chet* stands for that which is on a plane above nature, i.e., the **metaphysical Divine**."[12]

Since this letter is the initial letter in חן *chen*, the Hebrew word for "**grace**," it is also said to symbolize this quality. Combining this with the former quality, one could say it depicts God's grace in action. He writes, "Chet is phonetically similar to חטא *cheit*, sin."[13] So it can be used to describe the actions of man opposed to God. This letter is also said to be a symbol of "life," since the Hebrew word for life—chaim—begins with a ח *chet*. These are all important themes in the stories told in I & II Samuel. Biblically, since it follows 7 (the number of completion), the number 8 stands for the beginning of a new series—a new beginning. Since it goes beyond completion, it is called the number of super-abundance. Christians recognize it as the number of the "new birth in Christ."

Once, I & II Samuel were combined into a single book. Together, they tell the story of the birth of

Samuel, the last judge. More than that, they tell the story of a transition out of the old system of rulership under the judges into the period of the kings, beginning with Saul and David.

These two books truly portray a "new beginning" as Israel rejected the rule of God and cried out for a monarch, just like the ones who ruled the nations around them. Prior to that time, under the judgeship of Samuel, Israel experienced victory over the Philistines. But as Samuel grew old, the people rejected him, calling instead for a king. In the process, the people got Saul. As their first king, he exhibited many character flaws and public displays of sin. God soon rejected him as leader and anointed David to take his place.

Taken together, these activities reveal a theme of man's sinful life, played out against God's grace in action. With the death of Saul in II Samuel, the triumphs and troubles of David's life become focussed upon his throne and its perpetuation. In the seventh chapter, God graciously forms a covenant with David, promising him an eternal house with an eternal throne.

It is in the midst of David's sinful failures that God's grace brings the promise of a future Messianic Age. Even as sin and death bring the death of Absalom and the infant child of Bathsheba, God's grace in action brings a new beginning to the House of David.

I & II Kings *(Tet)*

The letter ט *tet* is something of an enigma. Its gematria is nine and its symbolism appears contradictory. Its two major meanings are first, a serpent and second, objective good.

I & II Kings were once combined into a single book, called in the Hebrew *Melechim* or, simply, "Kings." The stories of the kings are an amazing combination of good and evil. Certainly, the objective goodness of God presides over all their activities. But it is always intertwined with the evils of mortal men.

On the one hand, ט *tet* is said to stand for "objective good." This is thought to be true because the first time it appears in the Torah happens to be in the word *tov*, the Hebrew word for "good." Man longs for the "good" life. But as rabbi Munk writes:

> "Who can say what is good? Success is often ephemeral and prosperity corrupting, while setbacks and adversity often set the stage for advancement and triumph. Only God knows what is truly, objectively good for man."[14]

On the other hand, ט *tet* is the letter that stands for "the serpent" which is practically a universal symbol of evil. Even its shape suggests that accursed creature, with upraised tail on the right and head on the left.

Even its gematria of nine has a dual meaning. According to E. W. Bullinger, it is the number of finality and judgment. But it is also the number of blessing and the fruit of the spirit. For example, when Jesus first came to His people, He greeted them with nine blessings (Matt. 5:3-12). And in Galatians 5:22-23, the *"fruit of the Spirit"* is ninefold.

As might be expected then, the books of the Kings are especially laced with a mixture of good and evil. I Kings, for example, begins with David's decline in old age and the anointing of Solomon by Nathan the prophet. His reign would bring Israel to the material apex of its history.

But I Kings also opens with a plot. Adonijah proclaims that he will be the new king. He is surrounded by many men who support his accession to the throne. Unfortunately for him, Solomon has already taken the throne, with the blessing of God. His kingdom is firmly established and at that point, Solomon has Adonijah and his followers executed. Under Solomon's reign, the kingdom flourished. But the King, himself, made numerous mistakes, both in governance and in the affairs of his private life.

Perhaps the most noteworthy of Solomon's character qualities was his wisdom. Early in his reign, he prayed that might receive the gift of wisdom. God answered by giving him *"... a wise and an understanding heart."* His legacy of Proverbs and the stories of his wise rule are a spiritual treasure. Yet, during his reign, the kingdom was divided into Israel and Judah—as the ten northern tribes revolted. His monarchy ended under the cloud of God's chastening rebuke.

The histories of the kings are played out in the decline and fall of both Israel and Judah. As Israel is deported to Assyria and Judah is taken captive to Babylon, God makes a just end of both monarchies. But, in spite of their evil, His goodwill continues to maintain a righteous remnant in Israel.

Thus, we are given a picture that conforms perfectly with the letter ט *tet*. We find in the wisdom of Solomon, the objective good expressed in his willingness to be led by God's Spirit. But we also find evil, decadence, and finally, division.

I & II Chronicles *(Yod)*

The Hebrew letter ' *yod* stands for the number 10. It is said to represent God's creativity, as well as His deeper spiritual realities: "God created the universe with the letters ' *yod* and ה *hay* which form the Divine Name, יה *Yah*. With the letter ' *yod*, He created  the World to Come, while with the ה *hay*, He created This World."[15]

The books of I & II Chronicles were originally one scroll, the Hebrew title of which was *Dibere Hayamim* or, "The Words of the Days." We might call it "The Happenings of the Times." The Chronicles cover the period roughly between the time of II Samuel and II Kings. But where those books give a political history, the Chronicles give a spiritual or religious history. Hence, they are not simply a repetition of the books that precede them, but instead, offer a divine perspective on Israel's history.

Jewish tradition says that Ezra the priest was the author of these books. I Chronicles focuses on the royal line of David and his spiritual significance. II Chronicles concentrates on the history and influence of the Temple.

In view of the fact that the Jews believe ' *yod* to symbolize God's deeper spiritual realities, it is

interesting that both God's name יהוה *Hashem*
and the nation ישראל *Israel*, begin with a י *yod.*

The י *yod* is also the initial letter of יעקב *Jacob*,
who became Israel. The same is true of ישרון
Jeshurun, a diminutive form of "Israel," and יהודה
Judah, the tribe from which came the Messiah.
Thus, the main characters in the drama of the Old
Testament all begin with the initial י *yod.*

We would also add that the name of Jesus—ישוע
Jeshua, in Hebrew—begins with a י *yod.* Even the
name of God's holy city, ירושלם *Jerusalem*, begins
with this letter. Coincidence? Not if the sages of
Israel are right when they speak of it as "the
symbol of creation and the metaphysical."[16]

The books of the Chronicles, with their empha-
sis on the divine quality of Israel's history, are a
beautiful reflection of this theme.

Ezra, Nehemiah *(Kaf)*

The כ (ך) *kaf* has a numerical value of 20. It is said to be "the symbol of crowning accomplishment."[17] It is the first letter of the Hebrew word כתר *keter,* meaning "crown." Thus it is with wonder that we gaze  upon the crowning accomplishments of Ezra and Nehemiah—the rebuilding of the Temple after the Babylonian captivity and the restoration of the Mosaic Law. Originally, their history was recorded as a single book with two divisions called I & II Ezra.

Ezra tells the story of the waves of immigration into Jerusalem and the construction of the Temple. Nehemiah relates the rebuilding of the wall and the restoration of the Law of Moses.

Ezra speaks primarily of Judah's spiritual restoration, while Nehemiah is concerned with a geographic and political description of events. Together, they provide a composite picture of Israel's restoration and reformation. About the letter כ (ך) *kaf,* Rabbi Munk writes:

> "There are three crowns: ... the crown of priesthood, the crown of kingship, and the crown of Torah, but a fourth one ... the crown of a good name—is superior to them all."[18]

These crowns, he explains, refer to vessels in the Israel's ancient Temple. In Exodus 25:11, the ark is said to be topped by a *"crown of gold,"* referring to the crown of Torah. Verse 24 speaks of a similar crown atop the Table of Shewbread, the crown of kingship. The crown on the Altar of Incense illustrates the crown of priesthood. And the Menorah is a manifestation of the "crown of a good name." Notice that all these crowns stand in a completed Temple—the theme of Ezra and Nehemiah.

When the letter כ (ך) *kaf* appears at the end of a word, its form is changed. Instead of a bent כ *kaf*, it becomes a straightened letter that extends downward as a final ך *kaf*. It is said that the bent כ *kaf* speaks of the man who bends his baser impulses in order to control them. In the end, with divine assistance, he will rise "to the limit of his potential,"[19] as indicated by the straight ך *kaf*.

At the end of Nehemiah, the people of Israel had accepted the Law and the Priesthood; the Sabbath had been restored; and the people had been cleansed. Nehemiah 13:30-31—-the final two verses—relate this truth in brief form:

> *"Thus cleansed I them from all strangers, and appointed the wards of the priests and the Levites, every one in his business;*
> *"And for the wood offering, at times appointed, and for the firstfruits. Remember me, O my God, for good."*

Esther *(Lamed)*

Because its name, למד *lamed,* is related to למד *lamad*—which refers to both teaching and learning—this letter, ל *lamed*, is said to symbolize these activities.

The book of Esther is unique in Scripture, as the only book that does not directly mention God's name. But God's presence is clearly discerned to students of Esther's story, which is set in the palace of the Persian King Ahasuerus.

The king is revealed as an emotional man, rather vain and flippant. During a royal banquet at the palace of Susa, he wishes to show off his beautiful queen Vashti to the assembled guests. She refuses to appear and he is counseled to seek another queen, lest other women hear about what she did and themselves become insolent.

Somewhat later, Esther finds favor in the king's eyes at a royally-decreed "beauty pageant." Esther becomes Queen, but at her cousin Mordechai's urging, she does not reveal that she is Jewish. A little later, Mordechai hears about a plot to murder the king. He works through Queen Esther and the evil plan is revealed to the king. Mordechai's good deed is recorded in the palace records.

As the plot develops, a man named Haman is selected by the king for promotion. He is made captain of all the princes. But Mordechai, having knowledge of his evil character, refuses to bow to him. When Haman finds out that he is a Jew, he begins a year-long plot to rid the country of all Jews.

Important to the story is Haman's continual casting of lots (or Purim) during the entire time, in hopes of setting the perfect day for their mass killing. Through craft and guile, he even convinces the king to issue an edict saying that all Jews will be killed on one day, eleven months in the future.

However, the king has stumbled across the court record and learned about Mordechai's good deed. He wishes to honor him and asks Haman how this should be done. Haman thinks he is the one being honored and suggests a splendid public display. To Haman's embarrasment, he is commissioned to bestow public honor upon Mordechai!

Haman is so zealous to wreak his work upon the Jews that he has a huge gallows built, upon which he intends to make them a public spectacle, beginning with Mordechai.

As the planned fate of all Jews in the kingdom unfolds, Mordechai persuades Esther to take action. She reveals her nationality and bravely informs the king of Haman's plot. She makes a heartfelt plea for her people. Furious, the king hangs Haman on his own gallows and issues another decree, allowing the Jews to defend themselves on the day appointed for their execution.

The day following this joyous turn of events became a festival day on the Jewish calendar—Purim, named for the Persian term for "lots." From man's point of view, the casting of lots appears to be a random event. But a sovereign God controls the outcome of history.

From that day to this, Purim has been the Jewish festival of hilarity, featuring feasting, masquerades, parodies, plays, and noisemakers to drown out the despised name of the villain, Haman. It is the time when the enemies of the Jews are mocked. Joy is unbridled.

As we think about ל *lamed*, the letter of teaching and learning, we note that there is an enormous **lesson to be learned** from the historic event that led to this festival. The lesson has to do with anti-Semitism, or the belief that the Jews have somehow been forever cursed, to be replaced by righteous Gentiles. The lesson is this: **The Jews cannot be destroyed by making anti-Semitism the law of the land.**

During World War II, this lesson had to be learned all over again by the followers of Hitler.

After the war, Julius Streicher, Hitler's minister of propaganda, was sentenced to be hanged as a war criminal. As he ascended the gallows, he was heard to say, "Purim, 1946! Purim, 1946!"

All too well—but belatedly—he had learned the lesson of Purim. It is indeed appropriate that the book of Esther is represented by ל *lamed,* the letter that symbolizes teaching and learning.

Job *(Mem)*

The gematria of מ (ם) *mem* is 40, the number of probation, trial, or testing. The story of Job is that of a righteous man who is tested within the framework of conditions mandated by a sovereign God.

The מ (ם) *Mem* is said to be the letter symbolizing "the revealed and the concealed."[20] Rabbi Munk writes:

> "The open מ [*mem*] points to the obvious, openly revealed glory of God's actions. Figuratively, מ [*mem*] points upward to indicate God's sovereignty over us ... The closed ם [final *mem*] alludes to that part of the Celestial rule which is concealed from man and to which man submits instinctively and with perfect, innocent faith."[21]

The story of Job opens with a unique view of heaven and the throne of God. We have a rare revelation of the activity around God's throne. Job is described by God, Himself, as a *"perfect and upright"* man, *"one that feared God, and eschewed evil"* (Job 1:1).

He was a wealthy man with a large family and much livestock. In our terms, he could be thought of as a wealthy rancher. In the opening words of the book, Job is also revealed as the firm spiritual leader of his family.

But then, the scene shifts to heaven, and we overhear a conversation between God and Satan. Amazingly, the evil one appears there as a critic! God asks him what he thinks of Job, whom He has described in glowing terms. Satan answers that it is only God's protection that makes Job's faith function. He then challenges God to remove that protection, predicting that once evil begins to rain down on Job, he will curse God to His face.

The deed is then done. Satan is given his way. Destruction falls upon the house of Job. His children are killed; his property and livestock are ravaged; his servants are felled by enemies; and finally, Job is afflicted with boils—*"from the sole of his foot unto his crown"* (Job 2:7).

At that point, Job's test is underway. Chapters 3-37 feature a series of deep and painful discussions between Job and four of his friends, Eliphaz, Bildad, Zophar, and Elihu. In the process, their cycles of debate and defense detail Job's problems—the common problems of mankind.

Their questions reveal a paucity of wisdom about the motives and methods of a loving God. In grappling with Job's condition they accuse him— among other things—of hidden sin. Finally, Job falls prey to self pity. But as their discourses draw to a close, Elihu finally ends with a speech that exalts the greatness of God.

In the concluding chapters of the book, the Lord reveals Himself in a whirlwind, reminding Job of his lowly estate, contrasted with God's own incredible majesty. With his perspective restored, Job finally repents:

> *"I have heard of thee by the hearing of the ear: but now mine eye seeth thee.*
> *"Wherefore I abhor myself, and repent in dust and ashes"* (Job 42:5-6).

Job's friends also repent and make the appropriate sacrifices. In the end, Job's wealth and family are restored.

This marvellous story is perfectly illustrated by the open and closed מ (ם) *mem*. The open מ *mem*, with its bent posture is humble before Him, in recognition of His sovereignty. The closed ם *mem* depicts the purposes of God which are concealed from man. Job, the man of faith, finally realizes that his role is not to understand God, but to obey Him.

Psalms *(Nun)*

 *Nun* is called "the symbol of faithfulness, soul, and emergence."[22] Its gematria is 50. It is interesting that three times this number equals 150, or the number of Psalms. The **נ** (ן) *Nun* is the third of five Hebrew letters that have two forms. Rabbi Munk quotes a Jewish source who "... sees in the two forms of the **נ** (ן) *nun* a description of the Heavenly court. The bent **נ** *nun* symbolizes Hashem [God's Name] sitting on His Throne, while the stretched ן *nun* represents the angels standing before Him."[23]

Psalm One begins with a statement concerning the man of faith. He is promised blessing and fruitfulness:

> *"And he shall be like a tree planted by the rivers of water, that bringeth forth his fruit in his season; his leaf also shall not wither; and whatsoever he doeth shall prosper"* (Psalm 1:3).

As discussed at length in our book, HIDDEN PROPHECIES IN THE PSALMS, this man is Israel. The structure of Psalms is that of the Torah. That is, it is divided into five books, each of which bears a correspondence to the five books of Moses—Genesis through Deuteronomy.

The earthly journey of the man of faith is set in

the larger context of an enthroned ruler in the heavenlies:

> *"He that sitteth in the heavens shall laugh: the Lord shall have them in derision"* (Psalm 2:4).

Thus will the enemies of Israel come to their final judgment. This is the sovereign, enthroned God.

Psalm 110, the New Testament's most oft-quoted psalm, also carries *nun*'s message of the enthroned God:

> *"The Lord said unto my Lord, Sit thou at my right hand, until I make thine enemies thy footstool"* (Psalm 110:1).

The message of Psalms covers the entire gamut of Israel's struggle to emerge victorious in a world that is calculated to destroy them. Both in history and prophecy, the Psalms follow Israel through their long journey of faith and failure, deliverance and redemption, worship and apostasy. As they come to a close, there is a symphony of praise with the Messiah's return and the establishment of His Kingdom.

As the initial letter of נפילה *nefilah,* "downfall," *nun* is associated with defeat, followed immediately by salvation. This is the larger theme of Psalms. Israel's history is a repeated series of downfalls and deliverances that will be followed by redemption and eventual resurrection on a national level.

Proverbs *(Samech)*

The ם *Samech* is the letter that symbolizes "support, protection, and memory."[24] Its circular shape is said to serve as a reminder of God's supportive protection. The center of the circle is said to be a picture of the inside of the Tabernacle and the manifestation of the Shekinah glory of God.

This letter also symbolizes "memory." Of course, this book, of all the books in the Bible, is the book that is most often committed to memory as an aid to the wisdom of the believer's daily walk. The approximately 800 proverbs preserved here are attributed to Solomon who, according to I Kings 4:32, originated 3,000 proverbs and 1,005 songs.

The letter ם *samech* begins the Hebrew word סימן *siman,* which means, "a distinctive mark or sign." In its plural form, סימנים *simanim* (signs), it typifies the memory. It is recommended that one should "make *simanim* as study and memory aids."

A partial list of these memory aids would include gematria (numerical designations for Hebrew letters and words), acronyms, acrostics, contractions, and concept groupings. But especially, these memory aids are said to include **"proverbs, parables and allegories."** All such levels of learning go beyond the mere surface of Scripture, to reveal its deeper truths about the course of the spiritual man. Proverbs 1:5-6 says this exactly:

> *"A wise man will hear, and will increase learning; and a man of understanding shall attain unto wise counsels:*
> *"To understand a proverb, and the interpretation; the words of the wise, and their dark sayings"* (Proverbs 1:5-6).

Thus, the wise man—the spiritual man—will be equipped to resist temptation; to manifest obedience to God's word; and to grow in understanding. He will understand the more deeply-hidden interpretations of Scripture. Proverbs 1:7 is probably the most often quoted of Solomon's teachings:

> *"The fear of the Lord is the beginning of knowledge: but fools despise wisdom and instruction"* (Proverbs 1:7).

Throughout the book, wisdom is contrasted with foolishness. The fool is ultimately self-destructive, while the wise man experiences the blessing of God. More than that, the man of wisdom is protected and supported by the applied wisdom of God.

As mentioned above, ם *samech,* a circular letter representing God's encircling protection, is said to be an allusion to the Tabernacle—the dwelling place of God. Jews teach that spiritual Israel dwells in the protected center of the ם *samech.*

What a perfect picture of the wise man's progress.

He is supported and protected by God. Proverbs 3:26 states this eloquently:

> *"For the Lord shall be thy confidence, and shall keep thy foot from being taken."*

The gematria or numerical value of *samech* is 60. This number is said to encompass the larger part of the unit 100 and, therefore, stands for abundance and completeness. This is a perfect statement for the blessing of Proverbs.

Ecclesiastes *(Ayin)*

This book is written from the perspective of one who has had a long and difficult experience with life on earth. Solomon wrote the book, probably late in his life, after having personally witnessed a great many disappointments and missed  opportunities. Its perspective is earthly, as can easily be seen in its opening words:

> *"The words of the Preacher, the son of David, king in Jerusalem.*
> *"Vanity of vanities, saith the Preacher, vanity of vanities; all is vanity.*
> *"What profit hath a man of all his labour which he taketh under the sun?"* (Ecclesiastes 1:1-3).

The title "Ecclesiastes" comes from a Latin term that means, "a speaker before an assembled group." This, in turn, comes from the Greek term "ekklesia" referring to an assembled congregation.

In the Hebrew, the term is *Qoheleth* and is found only in this book, translated as "preacher." This is a book brought by an impassioned preacher. His fervent desire is to show us life on earth, *"under the sun,"* as it really is. He uses a very rational and logical method, based on careful observation.

Rabbi Munk writes, "The ע [*ayin*] is the letter of perception and insight, for its name עַיִן [*ayin*] means eye." [25]

Sight and insight are certainly the central features of this book. It deals with the ancient question, "What is life?" Amidst all its confusion, what seems to emerge is futility and meaninglessness. So the preacher opens with an observation: everything man does appears to be in vain. If that is the case, what can be the purpose of living?

He then proceeds to prove—both from Scripture and direct observation—that life is truly a procession of empty accomplishments. But having established this point, he turns his comments to the qualities of wisdom. It is wisdom that discerns the difference between life's futilities and God's purpose. As he brings his message to a conclusion, he discusses wisdom versus folly in much the same familiar style as in his Proverbs.

In Ecclestiastes 11:13-14, the preacher concludes that there is only one activity in life that is not in vain:

> "Let us hear the conclusion of the whole matter: Fear God, and keep his commandments: for this is the whole duty of man.
> "For God shall bring every work into judgment, with every secret thing, whether it be good, or whether it be evil" (Eccl. 11:13-14).

The eye of man sees only folly, but the eye of God shall ultimately decide the worth of man's every effort. Judgment is beyond man's capability; only God can see the truth of the matter.

The gematria of ע *ayin* is 70. Jewish scholars say that this number denotes spirituality. For example, they say that God has 70 names. Rabbi Munk writes, "Hashem [The Lord], Who has seventy names, gave the Torah, which has seventy names, to Israel, which has seventy names and which originated from seventy people who went down to Egypt with Jacob, and was chosen from among seventy nations, to celebrate seventy holy days in the year (52 Sabbaths and 18 Festivals, including the Intermediate Days of Pesach and Succos)."[26]

E. W. Bullinger says that 70 is the number associated with Jerusalem, "for the city kept its Sabbaths seventy years, while Judah was in Babylon (Jer. 35:11). And seventy sevens were determined upon it to complete its transgression, and bring in everlasting righteousness for it (Dan. 9:24)."[27] He also notes that 70 elders furnished Israel's great Tribunal, mentioned in Exodus, afterward called the Sanhedrin.

Jews believe that the "eye of God," is also suggested by the letter ע *ayin*. This, they say, is a figure of God's providence to His people. In Psalm 33:18-19, we find the perfect Scriptural basis for this observation:

> "Behold, the eye of the Lord is upon them that fear
> him, upon them that hope in his mercy;
> "To deliver their soul from death, and to keep them
> alive in famine."

In Ecclestiastes, the marked contrast between
man's limited vision and God's perfect view provides the driving force of the preacher's insightful
message. His sermon is clear—to bring meaning
to life, man must follow God's vision, not his own.

Song of Solomon *(Peh)*

The פ (ף) *peh*, symbol of "the mouth," is seen in the opening phrases of this book:

> "*The song of songs, which is Solomon's.*
> "*Let him kiss me with the kisses of his mouth: for thy love is better than wine*" (Song of Solomon 1:1-2).

The Song of Solomon, called in Hebrew *Shir Hashirim,* or "The Song of Songs," uses the richest possible language to illustrate the relationship between God and Israel, and to look forward to the same relationship between Christ and His bride, the Church.

The letter פ (ף) *peh* is another of the five Hebrew letters that is written in two forms, one of them being the open or final form. The Jewish Talmud speaks of the letter פ (ף) *peh* in relation to the closed mouth represented by the closed form פ *peh*, and the open mouth as seen in the open form ף *peh*.

Spiritually speaking, the function of the closed mouth is silence, representative of a time for learning Scripture. Conversely, the function of the open mouth is either to praise the Lord, or to spread His word to others who do not know about Him.

Its very title—"The Song of Songs"—ranks this as Solomon's best. It depicts the courtship and winning of a lowly shepherdess by King Solomon. It embodies the highest in poetic praise and emotional expression.

What better work in all the Old Testament to represent "the mouth"—the organ of eloquence and song?

Isaiah *(Tzaddi)*

Isaiah is represented by צ (ץ) *tzaddi*, the letter that denotes "righteousness." The central theme of the book is to be found in the name of the prophet who wrote it. Isaiah means "salvation is of the Lord." The word "salvation" is found 26 times in Isaiah, but only seven times in the works of all the other prophets. Of course, it is through the Lord's salvation that man finds righteousness or good standing in the sight of God.

In the book of Isaiah, the word for "righteous" or "righteousness" is found over 60 times. An excellent example appears in the first chapter:

> *"And I will restore thy judges as at the first, and thy counsellors as at the beginning: afterward thou shalt be called, The city of righteousness, the faithful city.*
> *"Zion shall be redeemed with judgment, and her converts with righteousness"* (Isaiah 1:26-27).

In Isaiah 46:13, the concepts of *righteousness* and *salvation* are combined:

> *"I bring near my righteousness; it shall not be far off, and my salvation shall not tarry: and I will place salvation in Zion for Israel my glory"* (Isaiah 46:13).

Toward the end of the book we find a statement that might be said to summarize the entire thrust and direction of Isaiah's prophecy:

> *"Thy people also shall be all righteous: they shall inherit the land for ever, the branch of my planting, the work of my hands, that I may be glorified"* (Isaiah 60:21).

In fact, all 66 chapters of Isaiah's prophecy may be said to be a discussion of righteousness; of man's inability to keep it, and of God's ultimate faithfulness in bringing man to a righteous state. It has been called a "miniature Bible."

The צ (ץ) *tzaddi* is the last of the five Hebrew letters that have both an ordinary and a final form. The צ *tzaddi* at the beginning or in the middle of a word is bent; at the end of a word, ץ *tzaddi* is elongated or straightened.

Pronouncing the name of the letter צ (ץ) *tzaddi* sounds like the Hebrew word for righteousness: צדיק *tzaddik.* In Hebrew, a man considered truly righteous is called a צדיק *tzaddik*. He is said to display the quality of his faith by his kneeling posture, just like the bent צ *tzaddi.* Like this letter, he is said to be bent in "humility."

The final ץ *tzaddi,* standing straight and tall, is said to "denote the final acceptance of a righteous person in the world to come."

That world—the world of the Messianic Kingdom—and the path to it are the very subjects of Isaiah's prophecy.

Jeremiah, Lamentations *(Koph)*

The ק *koph* is said to be the letter of "holiness and growth cycles."[28] It is said to be an allusion to God's holiness. Its association with holiness is easy to see, because it is the initial letter of the Hebrew word קדושה *kedushah*, the word for "holiness." The holiness of God is the model which man strives to attain. In the Torah, this idea is best expressed in Leviticus 19:1-2:

> *"And the Lord spake unto Moses, saying,*
> *"Speak unto all the congregation of the children of Israel, and say unto them, Ye shall be holy: for I the Lord your God am holy"* (Leviticus 19:1-2).

The ק *Koph* is also said to represent cycles of growth. Jewish sages say that it's relation to the word הקפה *hakafah*, "cycle," gives it this meaning. *Hakafah* comes from a Hebrew verb which means, "to go around."

It is said, "The seven-day week, climaxing in [Sabbath], the seven-year cycle climaxing in *Shemittah* (the Sabbatical year), the seven-*Shemittah* cycle leading to *Yovel* (the Jubilee Year), all remind the Jew that God created the world and continues to watch over it."[29]

During the year, the repetitive cycle of Sabbaths and festivals stands as a reminder to the Jew that

God provides a way for mankind to experience
cycles of growth that will ultimately bring a
faithful remnant to the position of original blessing. These cycles represent a fall and subsequent
rising. Rabbi Munk writes:

> "Adam did so when he let the serpent entice him into
> eating from the forbidden fruit in the Garden of Eden.
> Ever since, sin has been part of man's nature, with the
> result that God's Oneness is concealed ... But man's
> aberration is not permanent; eventually the cycle will
> return to its starting point, when—in Messianic times—
> Hashem [God] will be acknowledged by all mankind as
> the exclusive and absolute Ruler ... Every individual
> human being is challenged in his own life to make a
> spiritual cycle that will return him to his lofty ori-
> gin."[30]

Jeremiah and Lamentations were once considered a single book. They deal with the great
catastrophe of the Babylonian captivity and the
destruction of Jerusalem. For forty years, Jeremiah publicly condemned the apostasy of Judah,
warning the nation of God's impending judgment.
Because of his stance, the false priests and prophets of his day called for his death. But, because of
the intercession of certain public officials, he was
spared to continue his preaching. To say that he
was unpopular is a gross understatement.

In Jeremiah's day, the tribe of Judah had fallen
to an extremely low point in its spiritual progress.
He condemned the people for their empty profes-

sion of faith, saying that even the surrounding Gentiles had more faith in their false gods than Judah did in the one true God, who forbade Jeremiah to marry, as a sign of impending judgment. Finally, Jeremiah interceded for the people, but realized that their sin was so great that all he could do was lament their coming fall.

Judah was about to be dispossessed of its inheritance—at least for a time. Its people had reached the bottom of the cycle. Jeremiah 7:23 says it well:

> *"But this thing commanded I them, saying, obey my voice, and I will be your God, and ye shall be my people: and walk ye in all the ways that I have commanded you that it may be well unto you.*
>
> *"But they hearkened not, nor inclined their ear, but walked in the counsels and in the imagination of their evil heart, and went backward, and not forward"* (Jeremiah 7:23).

But, at the other end of the spectrum, Jeremiah's prophecy contains what must be one of the most encouraging and uplifting statements in all the Bible. It is the promise of a *"new covenant"* given in Jeremiah 31:31-33:

> *"Behold, the days come, saith the Lord, that I will make a new covenant with the house of Israel, and with the house of Judah:*
>
> *"Not according to the covenant that I made with their fathers in the day that I took them by the hand to bring them out of the land of Egypt; which my covenant they brake, although I was an husband unto them, saith the*

Lord:

"*But this shall be the covenant that I will make with the house of Israel; After those days, saith the Lord, I will put my law in their inward parts, and write it in their hearts; and will be their God, and they shall be my people*" (Jeremiah 31:31-33).

Thus, we see in Jeremiah and Lamentations, both the low point and the high point in the cycle of redemption. Even in the latter book, which is a funeral elegy for the destroyed city of Jerusalem, Jeremiah closes with a request for restoration:

"*Turn thou us unto thee, O Lord, and we shall be turned; renew our days as of old*" (Lamentations 5:21).

Jeremiah closes with a prayer that the times might turn, and that Judah might once again be elevated to a position of blessing. His prophecy foresees a cycle of blessing that will come in Messianic times. He looks forward to the time when his people will walk in holiness—in obedience to the Lord.

Ezekiel *(Resh)*

This letter, ר *resh*, stands for "the wicked" and "wickedness" in general. Jewish interpreters say that it comes by this designation because of its connection with the word רשע *rashah*, meaning "a wicked person."

Ezekiel 38-39 tells of a future invasion by Gog, chief *(rosh)* prince of Magog. *Rashah* may be more than a mere pun when compared to the pronunciation of modern *Rosh*—Russia. Throughout most of the years of this century, the northern nation has amply demonstrated the truth of its recent description as the "evil empire." Note that Gog and Magog are mentioned in Revelation 20, which also corresponds to ר *resh* (see page 159). In general, ר *resh* is said to be "the symbol of choosing between greatness and degradation." Rabbi Munk writes:

> "The wicked person from whom God turns away is one who willfully abandons the Torah and denies the sovereignty of God, one who intentionally becomes a non-believer."[31]

But he then goes on to say that in common interpretation, all is not lost in the life of such a man. In spite of deliberate wickedness, "yet a spark of good slumbers in every Jewish heart."[32] The choice must be made to repent.

The book of Ezekiel uses the term "wicked" or "wickedness" 42 times. The first use, in Ezekiel 3:17-19, is especially telling since it sets the theme of the prophecy and uses it seven times:

"Son of man, I have made thee a watchman unto the house of Israel: therefore hear the word at my mouth, and give them warning from me.

*"When I say unto the **wicked**, Thou shalt surely die; and thou givest him not the warning, nor speakest to warn the **wicked** from his **wicked** way, to save his life; the same **wicked** man shall die in his iniquity; but his blood will I require at thine hand.*

*Yet if thou warn the **wicked**, and he turn not from his **wickedness** nor from his **wicked** way, he shall die in his iniquity; but thou hast delivered thy soul"* (Ezekiel 3:17-19).

The Lord speaks to Ezekiel in a final discourse on the wicked in chapter 33. Here, the disobedience of the sinner is condemned, but in verse 19, the Lord gives Ezekiel, the watchman, a final hopeful note:

"But if the wicked turn from his wickedness, and do that which is lawful and right, he shall live thereby" (Ezekiel 33:19).

From that point forward, Ezekiel's prophecy takes a positive turn into the future, as it focuses upon the regathering of Israel and the rebuilding of the Temple.

Daniel *(Shin)*

The letter ש *shin* is said to be "the symbol of divine power and script—but also of corruption."[33] What a perfect symbol for the book of Daniel. His experience in the pagan court of Babylon becomes the story of a heroic faith under op-

pression. He and the other princes of Israel display a determined integrity to maintain their faith, even under persecution—to the point of death in the fiery furnace and the lions' den. The divine power that maintains them is in perfect contrast to the corruption of the Babylonian court.

Furthermore, his prophecy outlines *the times of the Gentiles* in a most remarkable way. Daniel is given the privilege of interpreting Nebuchadnezzar's dream of future great world empires: Babylon, Medo-Persia, Greece, and Rome—with its revival and extension in the far future.

But it is the seventh chapter of Daniel that provides the stable center of the prophecy. This is the vision of the Heavenly Father on His throne. He watches over the beast empires *"... for a season and time"* (v. 12). After that, the *"Son of man"* (v. 13) approaches the throne and receives His eternal kingdom. This is the divine power that gives order and perspective to all the other events that transpire.

The ש *shin,* symbol of שדי *Shaddai,* the omnipotent and omniscient provider God, is clearly seen in the book of Daniel. The prophet has an unshakable faith in God, and so, his life and witness are a testimony of God's שלום *shalom*—peace beyond all human understanding.

The ש *shin* is engraved on the Mezuza—a small container of Scripture found on the doors of every Jewish home. It is remarkable that Daniel refers to a "book" of life, which may correspond to a heavenly Mezuza, in Daniel 12:1:

> *"And at that time shall Michael stand up, the great prince which standeth for the children of thy people: and there shall be a time of trouble, such as never was since there was a nation even to that same time: and at that time thy people shall be delivered,* **every one that shall be found written in the book**" (Daniel 12:1).

This same "book" of life is mentioned in Revelation 21:27. As we pointed out, the ש *shin* also corresponds to the theme of Revelation 21 (see page 161). There we are told that on the gates of the New Jerusalem, the names of the twelve tribes are engraved (Rev. 21:12). Perhaps they are engraved on heavenly Mezuzas!

Twelve Minor Prophets (Tahv)

Because it concludes the Hebrew *Aleph-beit, tahv* is said to symbolize the perfect culmination of God's work. It is, therefore, the letter of "truth and perfection."[34] The ת *tahv* stands for the absolute, final analysis of things. It is typified in the

Hebrew word אמת *emet,* meaning "truth." Note that in *emet,* ת *tahv* is the final letter. This is said to imply that in the end, truth will prevail.

The twelve minor prophets provide exactly this kind of concluding perspective—from God's point of view. The first in the order is **Hosea**, prophet to the northern kingdom. He laments Israel's adultery and impending judgment. And he prophesies Israel's future restoration to God.

Then comes **Joel**, the prophet who defines the term, *"day of the Lord."* This day begins with the pouring out of God's wrath and culminates in the restoration of Judah, mentioned by Joel in his few verses. His name—*Yo'el*—in Hebrew means "Jehovah is God." It is fitting that this book emphasizes God's sovereign role in history.

Next we hear from **Amos**, who testifies, *"I was no prophet, neither was I a prophet's son; but I was an herdman, and a gatherer of sycamore fruit."* (Amos 7:14).

Things were so bad in Israel that even the prophets were corrupt—so God chose a common farmer to bring the burden of Israel. In graphic language, Amos details Israel's future judgment and the restoration that will ultimately follow—when Israel is replanted on the land.

Only 21 verses in length, the little book of **Obadiah** is a kind of broadside against Edom. The progeny of Jacob's twin brother, Esau, symbolize faithlessness and pride. One day, according to Obadiah, the territory of Edom will become the possession of Israel.

The prophet **Jonah** has a name which, in the Hebrew, means "dove," and is a Scriptural type of the Holy Spirit. Jonah is sent by God to bring repentance to the ungodly Gentile city of Ninevah. Though Jonah was reluctant, because the Ninevites were Israel's bitter enemies, God nevertheless forces Jonah to go. In the process, repentance comes to the evil city. The story is a beautiful illustration of God's grace in motion.

Micah, a prophet of the southern kingdom, addressed both Judah and Israel, probably writing in the time period prior to the Assyrian captivity of Israel in 722 B.C. Micah remembers the cause of downtrodden Judeans and tells them of the coming King. His message ends on a familiar note: *"Therefore I will look unto the Lord; I will wait for the God of my salvation ..."* (Micah 7:7).

The next minor prophet is **Nahum**. He prophesies the fall of Ninevah, the city which had
received salvation through Jonah about 50 years
earlier. His prophecy elucidates the certainty of
God's judgment on all the Gentiles who refuse to
receive God's grace.

Habakkuk means "embrace." This prophet
wrestles with the difficult questions concerning
God's sovereignty. How, he asks, can God use the
evil Babylonians—more evil than the Jews themselves—to be judges of God's chosen, holy people?
And how can the wisdom of the world be stronger
than the wisdom of the prophets? In his struggle,
Habakkuk remembers God's mercy and finally
trusts in God's salvation.

Like Joel, **Zephaniah** focuses on the *"day of the
Lord."* He speaks of its imminency and calls for
repentance. His scope goes farther than Joel's,
covering the whole earth. Like the other minor
prophets, he promises a final spiritual restoration to the world.

The name **Haggai** means "festive." This prophet
is associated with the fall and rising again of
God's Holy Temple. He even named the date of the
24th of Kislev, which several hundred years later
became the date of the Festival of the Temple
Dedication.

Zechariah has been called a miniature book of

Revelation for the Old Testament, because its visions so beautifully parallel those of the last book in the Bible. It deals with Israel's spiritual shortcomings and calls for repentance. Finally, it depicts the judgment of the nations and the coming of the Messiah to set up His kingdom.

The book of **Malachi** ends the Old Testament. The prophet recounts the sin of Israel's priesthood and its people. He then speaks of God's purifying judgment and the coming of the Lord. he concludes with his well-known discourse on the coming of a messenger to announce Messiah's arrival. The ultimate fulfillment of this prophecy tells of the coming of Elijah before the *"day of the Lord."*

For an in-depth study on the Minor Prophets, we suggest our book "THEY PIERCED THE VEIL AND SAW THE FUTURE."

Taken as a whole, the twelve prophets bring a message of firm hope and consolation. In the end, the Lord God will bring truth and perfection.

Thus we complete the 22 books. In the modern Masoretic text these have become 39 books. Isn't it amazing that during the diaspora of the last 2,000 years, the Tanach (Old Testament) has departed from its perfect 22-letter form, to assume the number of chastisement—39 stripes.

Chapter Six Notes:

1. F. F. Bruce, THE CANON OF SCRIPTURE (Downers Grove, Il., InterVarsity Press), p. 73.

2. Ibid., p. 75.

3. Flavius Josephus, *Against Apion*, Book 1, Paragraph 8.

4. Rabbi Michael L. Munk, THE WISDOM OF THE HEBREW ALPHABET (Brooklyn, N. Y., Mesorah), p. 43.

5. Ibid., p. 71.

6. Ibid., p. 90.

7. Ibid., p. 94.

8. Ibid., p. 95.

9. Ibid., p. 104.

10. Ibid., p. 105.

11. Ibid., p. 106.

12. Ibid., p. 112.

13. Ibid., p. 115.

14. Ibid., p. 119.

15. Ibid., p. 125.

16. Ibid.

17. Ibid., p. 133.

18. Ibid.

19. Ibid., p. 136.

20. Ibid., p. 143.

21. Ibid.

22. Ibid., p. 151.

23. Ibid.

24. Ibid., p. 159.

25. Ibid., p. 171.

26. Ibid., p. 175.

27. E. W. Bullinger, NUMBER IN SCRIPTURE (Grand Rapids, Kregel), p. 271.

28. Munk, WISDOM, p. 194.

29. Ibid., p. 196.

30. Ibid., p. 223.

31. Ibid., p. 199.

32. Ibid., p. 200.

33. Ibid., p. 207.

34. Ibid., p. 214.

Chapter Seven

The 27 Books of the New Testament and Their 27 Hebrew Letter Counterparts

Five of the 22 letters in the Hebrew alphabet (or *Aleph-beit* as it is properly known) have "final" forms, which are used only as the concluding letter in the spelling of a word. These five letters, when added to the 22, bring the *Aleph-beit* to a total of 27 letters ... the same as the number of books in the New Testament.

Can this be a coincidence? It seems unlikely since, as we have already noted, the Old Testament canon was structured around the Hebrew *Aleph-beit* from the time it was completed.

The New Testament completes—or finalizes—the Old Testament. The canon was closed with the addition of its 27 books. It is interesting to note that the 22 divisions of the Old Testament, along with the 27 books of the New Testament make a total of 49 parts to the whole of God's revelation to mankind. The number 49 is said to be the ultimate Divine perfection. Forty-nine is the product of seven sevens, and seven is the number of Divine perfection.

Though the Old Testament contains 39 books, some were combined in the first century, producing only 22 divisions. See comments on page 48.

Thus the infallible, inerrent Word of God is complete in every way. In fact, the Bible offers its own commentary upon this idea, in Revelation 22:18-19:

> *"For I testify unto every man that heareth the words of the prophecy of this book, If any man shall add unto these things, God shall add unto him the plagues that are written in this book:*
> *"And if any man shall take away from the words of the book of this prophecy, God shall take away his part out of the book of life, and out of the holy city, and from the things which are written in this book."*

With the addition of the five final letters—each of which speaks of the finalization of God's plan—the Bible is complete and perfect.

Matthew—Aleph

This is the book of the King. In its opening line Jesus is called *"Christ, the son of David, the son of Abraham."* He is announced as Messiah and King. He arrives in the land to systematically present the signs that confirm His Messianic claim.

The symbol under which this activity takes place is the letter א *aleph*, the symbol of God's unity and sovereignty. A close reading of this book reveals that Jesus was in complete control of every action that He took. As King, He proclaims the principles of the Kingdom and the power of the Messiah. The term *"kingdom of heaven"* is found 32 times in this book, but nowhere else in the entire New Testament.

But just as He is presented, so is He rejected, both by national Israel and numerous Gentile powers, all represented by their Roman overlords. His ministry concludes in Judea, turning away from the Temple and toward the world at large. He willingly gives up His life on the cross to redeem sinful mankind.

Matthew presents all His activity as perfectly controlled and fully completed. He made no mistakes. The letter א *aleph* is said to represent God's sovereign mastery over everything in His creation.

Mark—Beit

The ב *beit* is the letter of "blessing and creation," because it is the initial letter of the Hebrew words for those terms, ברכה *baracha* (blessing) and בריאה *bereshit* (creation). These two qualities are said to represent God's first work in Genesis.

The book of Mark presents the Lord as servant. He is shown acting in a direct, purposeful manner as He brings blessing to His people. Mark is filled with connecting terms, such as *"immediately," "forthwith,"* and *"straightway,"* giving Christ's work a sense of immediacy. In the original manuscript, the Greek words for these terms appear in Mark more often than in all the rest of the New Testament.

Perhaps the key verse is Mark 10:45, where his mission is announced: *"For the Son of man came not to be ministered unto, but to minister, and to give his life a ransom for many."*

The title *"Son of man"* refers to Jesus' role as servant and redeemer. In Mark, He is shown as the possessor of immense creative power, displaying the Messianic signs that validated his ministry. But more than that, He is specifically pictured as a man on a mission. He is on his way to give his life, so that the world might be blessed and redeemed.

Luke—Gimel

The author of this Gospel is known to have been a physician, possibly a Gentile. As he carefully brings together the elements of a document that records the humanity of Jesus, he displays the mind of an historian. The warmth of the narrative, coupled  with the carefully-drafted episodes of a compassionate Savior, continues the *"Son of man"* narrative begun by Mark, but emphasizes a Jesus who identifies with a lost mankind.

It is, therefore, quite interesting that ג *gimel* is known as the symbol of "kindness and culmination." Both of these qualities are reflected in the work of Jesus in bringing His plan of salvation to completion.

The ג *gimel* also has a gematria of three, which speaks of the Godhead:

> *"And the Holy Ghost descended in a bodily shape like a dove upon him, and a voice came from heaven, which said, Thou art my beloved Son; in thee I am well pleased"* (Luke 4:22).

As John baptizes Jesus, the heavens open and we are given a unique picture of Father, Son, and Holy Spirit. He is on a mission of grace and lovingkindness. Luke 19:10 says, *"For the Son of man is come to seek and to save that which was lost."*

John—Dalet

 As is well known, John presents Jesus as deity. The purpose of John is stated with great clarity in John 20:31: *'But these are written, that ye might believe that Jesus is the Christ, the Son of God; and that believing ye might have life through his name."*

In fact, the key word of this Gospel is *"believe."* The reader is urged to believe that Jesus is God. He is more than merely the provider of salvation; He is salvation, itself. He illustrated this by picturing himself as the door to the sheepfold. He is, therefore, the way of entry into salvation:

"I am the door: by me if any man enter in, he shall be saved, and shall go in and out, and find pasture" (John 10:9).

The letter ד *dalet,* as mentioned earlier, symbolizes "the door." Its shape is said to picture an open door, with a vertical doorpost and a horizontal lintel across the top.

Its gematria is four, the number of the Kingdom, of dimension and direction, as well as creation. In short, it is the word that suggests divinity or deity. John 1:1 says, *"In the beginning was the Word, and the Word was with God, and the Word was God."*

Acts—Hay

In its first chapter, the book of Acts outlines itself with great clarity: *"But ye shall receive power, after that the Holy Ghost is come upon you: and ye shall be witnesses unto me both in Jerusalem, and in all Judea and in Samaria and unto the uttermost part of the earth"* (Acts 1:8).

The ה *hay* is said to stand for the divinity and creative spirit of God. Its sound, corresponding to the English "h," is made simply by an exhalation of breath. This letter occurs twice in the name יהוה (Yahweh), translated "LORD" in the Old Testament. It speaks of the creative work of God and His redemptive work.

Jews also teach that this letter symbolizes repentance. So its main features are connected with the breath of God—His Holy Spirit—and the repentance of man.

Acts is the history of the Holy Spirit, Who moves the Gospel across the world, beginning in Israel. It is the story of the activation and validation of the Apostles, who established churches throughout the civilized world. When Paul met the Athenians he told them of a God who *"now commandeth all men every where to repent"* (Acts 17:30).

Romans—Vav

 The 1 *vav,* sixth letter of the Hebrew alphabet, has a numerical value of six. This number obtains its symbolic identity from the sixth day of creation—physical completion and mankind. It is man's number; the number of his physical and spiritual enterprise. Jews call it the "symbol of completion, redemption, and transformation."

Written by the Apostle Paul, Romans is the premiere work in Scripture on the subject of justification by faith, resulting in a transformed life. Its message follows the definition of 1 *vav:*

> *"For all have sinned and come short of the glory of God;*
> *"Being justified freely by his grace through the **redemption** that is in Christ Jesus"* (Romans 3:23-24).

But justification is only the beginning of another process often described in Romans. In one of its clearest statements, we find the very word used to describe 1 *vav:*

> *"And be not conformed to this world: but be ye **transformed** by the renewing of your mind, that ye may prove what is that good, and acceptable, and perfect, will of God"* (Romans 12:2).

Salvation does not require a changed life; rather, it changes lives.

I Corinthians—Zayin

Paul wrote this letter to early Christians living in a debauched and depraved society. In all the Roman empire, there was not a city as morally bankrupt as Corinth. Christians struggled to live a redeemed life there. Paul's letter was written as an aid to their victory.

From this perspective, it is especially compelling that ז *zayin* is called the letter of "spirit, sustenance, and struggle." This is a letter of discipline, in which Paul exerts powerful spiritual arguments against a number of different problems, including various kinds of immorality, abuses of spiritual gifts, and false theology.

The numerical value of ז *zayin* is seven. As such, it is said to represent man's struggle against outside forces. Every human being is said to be at the "focal point" of six directions: left, right, front, back, up, and down. The seventh point is at the center and is said to represent "the inner man, who is the object of all the forces, but is not part of them." Paul writes of this inner man:

"What? know ye not that your body is the temple of the Holy Ghost which is in you, which ye have of God, and ye are not your own?" (I Corinthians 6:19).

II Corinthians—Chet

 With a numerical value of eight, and since it is one beyond the perfect number seven, ח *chet* represents fullness or transcendence. Because it is the initial letter of the words חן *chen* (grace) and חיים *chayim* (life), it is also said to represent the qualities inherent in these terms.

The key verse in II Corinthians is 5:17:

"Therefore if any man be in Christ, he is a new creature: old things are passed away; behold, all things are become new" (II Corinthians 5:17).

This is a reference to the new birth in Christ, also referenced by the number eight, which is often called "the number of the new birth."

It is also the initial letter of חטא *cheit* (sin). This word, in fact, is pronounced very much like the name of the letter, itself. This book begins with Paul's defense of his ministry against certain false apostles who had attempted to discredit him. Paul expresses joy at the triumph of the true Gospel over this campaign of falsehood.

In a sense, this letter can be seen as a conflict between the grace of God and the sin of man, with God triumphant in the struggle.

Galatians—Tet

Jewish rabbis point out that in the books of Moses, the first occurrence of the letter ט *tet* appears in the word טוב *tov* "good," in Genesis 1:4. Because of this fact, it is taken to represent "good," or more specifically, "objective good." Goodness at this  level is far above the understanding of man, and can only truly be known by God. From man's point of view, His goodness manifests itself in both blessing and judgment.

Its numerical value is nine. Significantly, this is a number associated with both blessing and judgment. As to judgment, a good example is found in Haggai 1:11, in which God's judgment of the Jews is given in nine parts. As the number of blessing, there are two New Testament passages of note. The first is in Matthew 5:3-12, in which Jesus pronounces nine blessings upon Israel. The second is in Galatians 5:22-23, in which the *"fruit of the Spirit"* is given nine elements. Interestingly, one of them is *"goodness."*

Galatians is a complete discourse on the subject of law versus grace. Paul mentions, most appropriately, that blessings come through faith. He argues that faith is a good thing. In Galatians 5:18, he makes the point by saying, *"... it is good to be zealously affected always in a good thing ..."*

Ephesians—Yod

The ʼ *yod,* tenth letter of the Hebrew alphabet, has a numerical value of ten. It is called the letter of "creation and the metaphysical," or divinity. This is reckoned to be the case, since יהוה (Jehovah) begins with a ʼ *yod.*

Ephesians is especially noteworthy in that it opens with a statement of God's divine power and plan:

"Blessed be the God and Father of our Lord Jesus Christ, who hath blessed us with all spiritual blessings in heavenly places, in Christ:

"According as he hath chosen us in him before the foundation of the world, that we should be holy and without blame before him in love:

"Having predestinated us unto the adoption of children by Jesus Christ to himself, according to the good pleasure of his will" (Ephesians 1:3-5).

Ephesians deals with the metaphysical in express terms. Chapter 1, verse 9 says, *"Having made known unto the mystery of his will, according to his good pleasure which he hath purposed in himself."* The mystery of which Paul writes is the position of the believer who is safe in Christ. In Eph. 3:3-4, he refers to it as the *"mystery of Christ."* In verse 9, he calls it *"the fellowship of the mystery."* Truly, this letter expounds the metaphysical and creative truth of God.

Philippians—Kaf

The כ (ך) *kaf* is said to be the letter of "crowning accomplishment." It is the initial letter of the Hebrew word כתר *keter* (crown). It also has a final form, which we will discuss on page 260.

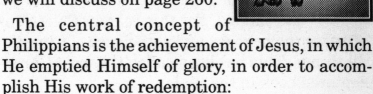

The central concept of Philippians is the achievement of Jesus, in which He emptied Himself of glory, in order to accomplish His work of redemption:

> "Let this mind be in you, which was also in Christ Jesus:
>
> "Who, being in the form of God, thought it not robbery to be equal with God:
>
> "But made himself of no reputation, and took upon him the form of a servant, and was made in the likeness of men:
>
> "And being found in fashion as a man, he humbled himself, and became obedient unto death, even the death of the cross.
>
> "Wherefore God also hath highly exalted him, and given him a name which is above every name" (Phil. 2:5-9).

In his opening explanation of כ (ך) *kaf,* Rabbi Munk says, "There are three crowns … the crown of priesthood, the crown of kingship, and the crown of Torah, but a fourth one—the crown of a good name—is superior to them all." Surely, the crowning accomplishment of Jesus Christ is higher than any other in the history of mankind.

Colossians—Lamed

Paul wrote Colossians to counter a heresy called "gnosticism"—the doctrine of special knowledge. The life of Jesus Christ had been devalued, in favor of intellectual speculations, mystical visions, rituals, and regulations. For this reason, Colossians stresses the primacy and sufficiency of Christ in all things. This has been called the most Christ-centered book in the Bible.

The ל *lamed* is the Hebrew letter associated with "teaching and purpose." It is a tall, majestic letter, towering above the others. Because of that, it is said to symbolize the King of kings. This is further stressed because ל *lamed* is flanked in the alphabet by מ *mem* on one side and כ *kaf* on the other. This arrangement forms the word, מלך *melech,* or "king."

The ל *lamed* also resembles the Hebrew word for learning and teaching: למד *lamad.* As related to Colossians, the message of ל *lamed* is clear, since this book focuses on the subject of "teaching" about Christ:

"Beware, lest any man spoil you through philosophy and vain deceit, after the tradition of men, after the rudiments of the world, and not after Christ.

"For in him dwelleth all the fullness of the Godhead bodily" (Colossians 2:8-9).

I Thessalonians—Mem

Because of its open and closed forms, מ (ם) *mem* is called the "symbol of the revealed and the concealed." As pointed out under "Colossians," מ *mem* is the initial letter of the Hebrew word מלך *melech,* or "king." For this reason, it speaks of God's kingship and dominion. Therefore, מ *mem* symbolizes God's truths, some of which are clearly revealed to man, and some of which are concealed. On page 261, we will further discuss the final ם *mem.*

How appropriate that this letter should represent I Thessalonians, since it expounds the pre-tribulational rapture of the church. This doctrine is presented to the Thessalonians as a comforting hope. They are clearly told that they need not fear the *"day of the Lord,"* since it is not for those who hold to the hope of Christ's return for His church.

The pre-tribulational catching away of the church is revealed with blessed clarity for those whom the Spirit leads in Scriptural understanding. But for some, this doctrine is a contradictory muddle of irreconcilable facts. Many scornfully deride a "secret rapture," which they say can't be found in Scripture. To them, it is concealed.

II Thessalonians—Nun

 This epistle clearly expounds the relationship between the *"day of the Lord,"* and the church. Certain false teachers had attempted to convince the Thessalonians that the day of judgment had already begun, and that they would experience the wrath of God. Paul had already taught that they wouldn't go through the Tribulation. This letter is meant as a reinforcement of that earlier personal instruction.

Among other things, נ (ן) *nun* is said to symbolize "faithfulness" and has two forms. The bent נ *nun* pictures humble submission to God's will; the elongated ן *nun* typifies the righteous man, standing upright before God in the day of judgment. We will look further at the final ן *nun* on page 262.

The נ (ן) *nun* is said to typify the hope of redemption and future resurrection. Second Thessalonians is written to a fellowship whose spiritual progress greatly pleases Paul. Of them, he says, *"... your faith groweth exceedingly"* (II Thes. 1:3).

This epistle is written to comfort and restore the reader. It is based upon, *"... the coming of our Lord Jesus Christ, and by our gathering together unto him"* (II Thes. 2:1). And it is in this hope that we find the very meaning of the letter נ (ן) *nun*.

I Timothy—Samech

The ס *samech* is the letter of "support, protection and memory." Since it has the shape of a circle, it metaphorically suggests the surrounding protection of God, with the believer carefully kept in the center. Rabbis say that it alludes to the Tabernacle, with Israel at its center.

This set of meanings perfectly fits I Timothy which, along with II Timothy and Titus, are devoted to outlining the duties and obligations of a pastor in relation to his congregation. The metaphoric meaning of ס *samech* almost exactly outlines these duties. As Paul writes:

> *"If thou put the brethren in remembrance of these things, thou shalt be a good minister of Jesus Christ, nourished up in the words of faith and of good doctrine, whereunto thou hast attained"* (I Timothy 4:6).

Paul urges Timothy to support and protect the faith of the early church by helping them to remember the doctrine of the Apostles.

The ס *samech* also stands for סימנים *simanim,* or "signs" to be used as an aid to the memory while studying Scripture. Paul writes, *"Till I come, give attendance to reading, to exhortation, to doctrine"* (I Timothy 4:13). In short, Paul asks Timothy to support his flock, and to be an aid to their memory of Scripture.

II Timothy—Ayin

The ע *ayin* is the letter of "sight, insight and spirituality." It has a numerical value of 70, a number denoting spirituality. At the heart of Paul's second letter to Timothy lies a Scripture passage that seems to encompass all these qualities:

"But continue thou in the things which thou hast learned and hast been assured of, knowing of whom thou hast learned them;

"And that from a child thou hast known the holy scriptures, which are able to make thee wise unto salvation though faith which is in Christ Jesus.

"All Scripture is given by inspiration of God, and is profitable for doctrine, for reproof, for correction, for instruction in righteousness:

"That the man of God may be perfect, thoroughly furnished unto all good works" (II Timothy 3:14-17).

The Hebrew word ע *ayin* means "eye." As such, it denotes the vision and perception of both God and man. In the latter, it also typifies the "tempted eye," that can lead to apostasy. In II Timothy 4:2, Timothy is urged to confront such errant thinking:

"Preach the word; be instant in season, out of season; reprove, rebuke, exhort with all longsuffering and doctrine" (II Timothy 4:2).

Titus—Peh

The פ (ף) *peh* is called the "symbol of speech and silence." It stands for פה *peh,* or "mouth." This is the fourth of five Hebrew letters that have both a normal and a final form. The closed פ *peh* symbolizes  silence; the open ף *peh* indicates speech. There is an appropriate time for each of these activities. The final, open ף *peh* will be further discussed on page 263. Paul's letter to Titus is the last of the "pastoral epistles." In Titus 1:11, Paul urges Titus to rebuke those who speak false doctrine:

*"Whose **mouths** must be stopped, who subvert whole houses, teaching things which they ought not, for filthy lucre's sake."*

On the positive side Paul instructs Titus to make known the sound doctrine that he has been so carefully taught:

*"But **speak** thou the things which become sound doctrine"* (Titus 2:1).

*"Sound **speech**, that cannot be condemned; that he that is of the contrary part may be ashamed, having no evil thing to say to you"* (Titus 2:8).

*"These things **speak,** and exhort, and rebuke with all authority"* (Titus 2:15).

*"To **speak** evil of no man ..."* (Titus 2:2).

*"This is a faithful **saying**, and these things I will that thou affirm constantly ..."* (Titus 3:8).

Philemon—Tzaddi

The צ (ץ) *tzaddi* stands for righteousness and humility. Its name bears a close resemblance to צדיק *tzaddik,* or "righteous person." It is the last of five Hebrew letters that have two forms. The normal, bent צ *tzaddi* is said to suggest a man on bended knee; the final, straight ץ *tzaddi* stands for the acceptance of the righteous man in the world to come. More on the final form is given on page 264.

Paul's epistle is really only a brief note to explain that Philemon's runaway slave, Onesimus, has now received the message of the gospel and is safe in Christ. Paul implores Philemon to accept his slave's return, who, having been born again, is now trustworthy, profitable and obedient. Paul asks that Philemon receive him:

> *"Not now as a servant, but above a servant, a brother beloved, specially to me, but how much more unto thee, both in the flesh, and in the Lord ..."* (Philemon 16).

Onesimus had rebelled against Philemon, but was now humble and ready to take his place in that household once again. He had become a *tzaddik.* Furthermore, Paul writes that he, himself, is a prisoner and bondslave of Jesus Christ— a humble and righteous man.

Hebrews—Koph

The ק *koph* is the letter of "holiness and growth cycles." It is said to allude to God's קדושה *kedusha,* or "holiness." Also, it relates to the word הקפה *hakafah,* or "cycle." The idea is that all things proceed in cycles. On this note, Jews teach that man began in the perfection of the garden of Eden and will return to paradise in the Messianic era.

The book of Hebrews lays stress on the holiness of Christ, who is pictured as the perfect sacrifice:

"Neither by the blood of goats and calves, but by his own blood he entered in once into the holy place, having obtained eternal redemption for us" (Hebrews 9:12).

The writer to the Hebrews also urges that they,

"Follow peace with all men, and holiness, without which no man shall see the Lord" (Hebrews 12:14).

Holiness implies dedication to, and involvement in, the redemptive plan of God. It also speaks of the completion of that plan. In this case, the reference would be to the acceptance of the new covenant by the Hebrews. This would be the completion of a growth cycle:

" ... Behold the days come, saith the Lord when I will make a new covenant with the house of Israel and with the house of Judah" (Hebrews 8:8).

James—Resh

The epistle of James deals with the subject of the believer's testing in an evil world. It speaks of a faith that not only endures testing, but also produces the works of right-eousness that are so valuable to a degenerate world system.

It also deals with the judgment of the wicked. James sets the tone of his letter with a definitive statement:

> *"Let no man say when he is tempted, I am tempted of God: for God cannot be tempted with evil, neither tempteth he any man."*
>
> *"But every man is tempted, when he is drawn away of his own lust, and enticed"* (James 1:13).

In the positive sense, the act of being tempted would refer to a trial or approval; in the negative, to the activity of "the tempter," or the devil. Through all the trials, faith serves with steadfast endurance. Faith, according to James, can be observed through one's works.

In this context, it is interesting that ר *resh* is the letter associated with "choosing between great-ness and degradation." It stands for the wicked person, who has fallen prey to his own inner weaknesses and will one day be judged if he does not repent.

I Peter—Shin

The ש *shin* denotes "divine power ... but also corruption." Jewish commentators link this letter to the most powerful of all God's names: שׁדי *Shaddai*, the omnipotent God and master of the universe.

The ש *shin* also has a dark connotation. The sages of Israel teach that because of its close proximity to ק *koph* and ר *resh* in the *Aleph-beit*, it stands for שׁקר *sheker,* or "falsehood."

I Peter was written from *"Babylon"* (I Peter 5:13), to the believers in Asia Minor. Most expositors believe that the city name given by Peter is a code word for Rome, since it is known that he was martyred there in about A.D. 65 or 66. This epistle was probably written just prior to the great persecutions under Nero, which began in A.D. 64. For Christians in the Roman Empire, it was a time of great trial.

Peter's purpose in writing was to give his readers the proper perspective on suffering and persecution, so that they would be able to endure. The theme of his letter is "suffering under the false world system." The key statement of this idea is in 4:12, *"But rejoice, inasmuch as ye are partakers of Christ's sufferings ... "* God's power will see the believer through to the end.

II Peter—Tahv

The ת *tahv* is the letter of "truth and perfection." It is symbolized by the final letter of the Hebrew word for truth, אמת *emet*. This, the final letter of the *Aleph-beit*, signifies the completion and perfection of God's plan. Since ת *tahv* is at the end of the word, it is said to symbolize man's final destination.

It is fascinating that II Peter reflects this exact idea. Peter argues against the heresies of false teachers, first by recalling the truth of Christ's transfiguration experience. Then, he points out that, *"We have also a more sure word of prophecy ..."* (II Peter 1:19). He contrasts the truth of Scripture against the teachings of men whose motives are less than pure—who preach for money and power. Finally, he points out that in the last days, people would actually scoff at the idea of Christ's coming.

But in the end, he says, *"the day of the Lord will come as a thief in the night ..."* (II Peter 3:10). He writes not only of the beginning of this day, but its conclusion: *"Nevertheless, we, according to his promise, look for new heavens and a new earth, wherein dwelleth righteousness."*

This is truth, and this is perfection.

The Five Final Forms

As pointed out several times in this book, there are five Hebrew letters that have two different forms. Their normal form is used at the beginning or in the middle of a word. These letters are כ *kaf,* מ *mem,* נ *nun,* פ *peh,* and צ *tzaddi.*

Their final forms are used when the letter appears at the end of a word. These final forms are ך *kaf,* ם *mem,* ן *nun,* ף *peh,* and ץ *tzaddi.* In general, these final forms are interpreted as representing the final outcome of each letter's symbolic meaning. That is, they are prophetic in nature and look toward the end of God's redemptive process. The normal letter is said to represent the spiritual man's present struggles; the final is his destination.

Added to the 22 normal letters, they bring the total number of letters in the Hebrew *Aleph-beit* to 27, the exact number of books in the New Testament. Since they represent the final outcome of God's plan, it seems fitting that they should be placed beyond the end of the *Aleph-beit.* As we proceed to the conclusion of the New Testament, we find that the correspondence of meaning between each letter and its representative book continues in a remarkable way.

I John—Final Kaf

The final ך *kaf* is an elongated letter that is said to "stand straight," indicating self-control. It speaks of the man who, with God's help, has finally overcome his baser impulses and stands straight before God. The theme of the letter in general is "crowning achievement."

The theme of I John is "fellowship with God." John writes eloquently about walking in God's light and abiding in His love. Following the theme of "crowning achievement," John writes:

> *"Beloved, now are we the sons of God, and it doth not yet appear what we shall be: but we know that, when he shall appear, we shall be like him; for we shall see him as he is"* (I John 3:2).

What a beautiful picture of the believer's final achievement! The theme continues in chapter 4, verse 17, *"Herein is our love made perfect, that we may have boldness in the day of judgment ..."* Achieving one's spiritual potential is the exact meaning in the final *kaf*. Chapter 5, verse 4 is an even stronger statement of this idea. *"For whatsoever is born of God overcometh the world ..."*

I John is a beautiful statement of the believer's final status before God.

II John—Final Mem

The final ם *mem* is a closed figure. It stands for "the concealed." It typifies the sovereignty of God that is unknowable by man, and to which man submits by faith.

There is much of a concealed and mysterious nature in John's second epistle. To begin with, verse 1, opens with a salutation to *"the elect lady and her children,"* whose identity is unknown. Some scholars have suggested that the reference is to a specific woman. Others have said that they speak figuratively of a local church. Still others think the letter is addressed by the Holy Spirit to the church at large; the entire body of believers throughout the Church Age.

The letter closes in verse 13, with another cryptic note: *"The children of thy elect sister greet thee."* Is John referring to a specific woman, a sister church, or to a relationship between all the churches that would ever exist?

One thing is certain. John's message urges his readers to walk in love and avoid the doctrine of false teachers. In verse 12, he expresses a desire *"to come unto you, and speak face to face, that our joy may be full."* It is as though he is saying, "One day, the concealed will be revealed."

III John—Final Nun

III John is addressed to *"the well-beloved Gaius, whom I love in the truth."*Gaius' generosity is contrasted with the self-serving and malicious behavior of a man called Diotrephes.

The normal **נ** *nun* represents the spiritual man, "who submits humbly to God's will." The final, straightened **ן** *nun* is said to represent the man who stands upright before God in the final day of judgment.

Such a man is the godly Gaius. John writes:

*"For I rejoiced greatly, when the brethren came and testified of the truth that is in thee, even as thou **walkest** in the truth.*

*"I have no greater joy than to hear that my children **walk** in truth"* (III John 3-4).

Nun generally typifies "faithfulness"—both that of God and of man. Gaius is reminded by John to keep the faith and to avoid evil influences, while following the goodness of God.

Like II John, this letter closes with a curious note of passionate longing. In verse 14, John writes, *"But I trust that I shall shortly see thee, and we shall speak face to face."*

The thought is that soon, the faithful will be gathered in a joyful reunion.

Jude—Final Peh

The brief epistle of Jude is a resounding condemnation of all those false teachers who have ever contradicted the express plan of God. In the most unmistakable way, it judges the loud-mouthed and errant verbalizations of all those who have ever preached a false gospel.

The פ (ף) *peh* is the letter of the mouth and of speech. In its normal closed form, פ *peh* represents silence. In its open final form, ף *peh* typifies speech. It teaches that there is "a time for silence and a time for speech." Jude writes in verse 8 that the false teachers "... *speak evil of dignities.*" That is, they blaspheme the authority of God. In verse 10, he writes that they, "... *speak evil of those things which they know not.*" He calls them, "... *Raging waves of the sea, foaming out their own shame ...*" Here, they can almost be seen foaming at the mouth. Following the theme, Jude writes:

> *"These are murmurers, complainers, walking after their own lusts; and their mouth speaketh great swelling words, having men's persons in admiration because of advantage"* (Jude 16).

At the heart of his letter, Jude reminds his readers that the Lord is coming to judge these false teachers. Their mouths will one day be shut.

Revelation—Final Tzaddi

The letter **צ** (**ץ**) *tzaddi* is said to symbolize "the righteousness of God and devout human beings." The pronunciation of this letter's name is very close to the Hebrew word for "a righteous man" (see the comment under "Philemon.")

In its normal, bent form **צ** *tzaddi* almost has the appearance of a man on bended knee. The final **ץ** *tzaddi* is straightened and is said to "denote the final acceptance of a righteous person in the world to come."

How perfectly this reflects the theme of the book of Revelation! This wonderful book concludes the Church Age and the judgment of the world. The Righteous Judge, the Lamb, comes forth and brings *"the times of the Gentiles"* to an end.

Revelation also depicts Christ's Second Coming to defeat earth's armies. The system of satan is destroyed at the judgment of the *"great white throne."*

Finally, the eternal state is established. The *"New Jerusalem* "and the *"... new heaven and ... new earth"* are brought into being. At long last, eternal righteousness is established and the righteous live in fellowship with God forever after.

Chapter Eight

Matthew Reveals a Torah Design

We have come across an absolutely fantastic design in the first Gospel of the New Testament.

Matthew (being a Levite) was given the opportunity to write the first book of our New Testament. One of his relatives, Moses (also a Levite) wrote the first book of the Old Testament. In fact Moses wrote five books: Genesis, Exodus, Leviticus, Numbers, and Deuteronomy. And, as Matthew unfolds the life of Christ to the Jewish people, he divides his Gospel into five divisions—corresponding with the five books of Moses!

Matthew originally wrote his Gospel in the Hebrew language. In the fourth century, Jerome said that the Hebrew original of Matthew was kept in a library at Caesarea. The original has long since disappeared. Fortunately, Matthew was translated into Greek during the first century so that copies could be distributed around the world.

It was not difficult for Matthew to use the framework of the Torah (Law) in laying out his book, because Jesus actually lived out his life and ministry in the order of those five books.

Matthew's use of the Torah or Penteteuchal design is not unique. A few years ago, we learned that the Psalms are also divided into five divisions, corresponding with the five books of Moses. Now we learn that, to introduce this new extension of Abraham's Covenant of Grace, Matthew gives us five Torah-like divisions of the life of Christ. Jesus' ministry and messages followed the framework of Genesis, Exodus, Leviticus, Numbers, and Deuteronomy.

The five Divisions of Matthew are as follows:

The Genesis Chapters—Matthew 1-7
The Exodus Chapters—Matthew 8-11
The Leviticus Chapters—Matthew 12-17
The Numbers Chapters—Matthew 18-20
The Deuteronomy Chapters—Matthew 21-28

This appears to be the fulfillment referred to by Jesus: *"I have not come to destroy the law, but to fulfill it."* We find such a fulfillment—in design—in the Gospel of Matthew.

The Genesis Chapters
Matthew 1-7

The first seven chapters of Matthew correspond with the book of Genesis. Matthew opens the geneology of Jesus Christ with the words, *"The book of the generation of Jesus Christ."* This follows the design in the book of Genesis where we have the generations of Adam. This neat little summary at the beginning of Matthew implies that we are linking the structure of the first New Testament book with the structure of Genesis.

The Sermon on the Mount

Each division of Matthew contains a key discourse. In this first section, we have the "Sermon on the Mount." In it, Jesus pronounced a nine-fold blessing and restated the qualities of the Abrahamic Covenant. He reminded everybody where they came from and how the kingdom would relate to them personally in terms of their own behavior.

The Second Adam

Now, let's look at the birth of Christ and note how His birth corresponds to the creation of Adam. Jesus was the *"seed of the woman"* promised to Eve. What Adam lost, Jesus will restore!

The Sojourn in Egypt

As an infant, Christ was taken into Egypt for safety. This corresponds to the story of Israel in its infancy as given in Genesis! Joseph was sold into Egyptian slavery. Jesus was also betrayed and sold for a few shekels of silver. It was Joseph's destiny to become the Governor of the land. He was a prophetic picture of Christ, Who, having been rejected, becomes the Savior of Gentiles.

As the story of Joseph concludes, he sends a message to his father, Jacob, that he is alive. He invites him to come down into Egypt—which Jacob did with all 70 relatives. In like manner, we have the story of Christ being taken into Egypt at a young age, fulfilling the prophecy which says, *"Out of Egypt have I called my son."*

The Temptation of Christ

The Temptation of Christ, related in the opening chapters of Matthew, corresponds to the temptation of Adam and Eve in the garden of Eden:

> *"Then was Jesus let up of the Spirit into the wilderness to be tempted by the devil"* (Matthew 4:1).

The devil's temptation to Eve came in a beautiful garden under perfect conditions. But the temptation of the *"seed of the woman"* came in a wilderness under the most difficult conditions. This time, however, the temptation was resisted and conquered.

The Exodus Chapters
Matthew 8-11

The second division of Matthew (8-11) follows the story-line of Exodus—the crossing of a sea, a group drowning in the waters, and miracles performed—only to be followed by unbelief and murmuring. Matthew 8:23-27 gives us the story of Jesus taking a boat across Galilee. During the crossing, He laid down, went to sleep, and a storm arose. The disciples woke Him and said, *"Lord, save us: we perish."* Jesus arose, rebuked the wind, and said, *"Why are ye fearful, O ye of little faith?"* (Matthew 8:25-26). This story corresponds to a story in Exodus—the crossing of the Red Sea.

Drowning in the Sea

Upon arriving in the country of Gadara, Jesus was approached by two who were possessed with devils. Note that Jesus cast the demons into a herd of swine, which violently ran down the steep slopes and drowned in the waters of Galilee. The story corresponds to the drowning of Pharaoh's army in the midst of the Red Sea. The comparison of Matthew 8-11 to Exodus is apparent.

Miracles Performed

Also in these chapters, we have the performance of miracles—we have healings, the restoration of life, sight, speech, all sorts of miracles—corresponding to the miracles related in Exodus. Note, however, that the people suffered from a chronic case of unbelief in Moses' day. And, in like manner, the message of Christ was rejected, whereupon, Jesus leveled a scathing rebuke against unbelief:

"Woe unto thee, Chorazin! Woe unto thee, Bethsaida! For if the mighty works, which were done in you, had been done in Tyre and Sidon, they would have repented long ago in sackcloth and ashes" (Matthew 11:21).

This unbelief corresponds to Exodus where there was a constant murmuring.

Jesus' Second Sermon

This Exodus division has its discourse as well. In Matthew 10, Jesus commissioned the twelve apostles. Before He sent them out, Jesus gave them a lengthy discourse on apostleship:

"Go ... Provide neither gold, nor silver, nor brass in your purses, Nor scrip for your journey, neither two coats, neither shoes, nor yet staves ..." (Matthew 10:5-10).

What He is saying here is the same message we have in the book of Exodus. Stay away from the Gentiles. Throughout the wilderness journey, God provided for Israel. Under Moses, the people had water to drink, quail to eat, and manna to sustain them. Their clothes and shoes never wore out.

The Kingdom Is at Hand

The message of these twelve disciples was, *"The kingdom of heaven is at hand!"* Yet, the people did not believe it. That is the message of Matthew and that was the message of Exodus as well. The kingdom lay before them. It was at hand and yet the people rejected it.

The Leviticus Chapters Matthew 12-17

Matthew 12-17 deals with the law of the Sabbath—corresponding with the theme of Leviticus. Many stories are given about events that happened on the Sabbath day. For example, Jesus has a confrontation with the Pharisees over the disciples plucking corn and eating it on the Sabbath (12:1-8). This is the same kind of theme found in Leviticus. The law of the Sabbath is given in Leviticus 23:3:

> *"Six days shall work be done: but the seventh day is the sabbath of rest, an holy convocation; ye shall do no work therein: it is the sabbath of the Lord in all your dwellings."*

The main theme in these Leviticus chapters of Matthew's Gospel centers around the message that Christ is the Lord of the Sabbath.

Parables of the Kingdom

Beginning in Matthew 13, Jesus delivered His third discourse—the parables of the Kingdom. This also corresponds with the message of Leviticus. Some 1,500 years earlier, the Jews in

the wilderness were also anticipating a kingdom—the Promised Land. But the people rejected the opportunity and stayed in the wilderness for 40 years.

In Matthew, Jesus offered the kingdom of heaven,
only to be rejected. Instead of sitting upon a
throne, He hung upon a cross. Instead of wearing
a golden diadem, He wore a crown of thorns. Jesus
was ultimately rejected and the Kingdom had to
wait for a future generation.

Feeding the Multitudes

In these chapters, Jesus fed five thousand on
one occasion and another four thousand a few
days later. This relates back to the wilderness
journey as well. In the wilderness the Lord fed the
people with quail, manna, and water from the
rock.

The Transfiguration

The conclusion of the Leviticus section of Matthew is very exciting. Chapter 17 ends this section with the transfiguration. Matthew 17:1 says:

*"And after six days Jesus taketh Peter, James, and
John his brother, and bringeth them up into an high
mountain apart."*

This is the ultimate conclusion to the parables of
the kingdom. It is a long range view of that
kingdom.

When Jesus was on top of the mount, his face shone as the sun. This corresponded to Moses on top of Mount Sinai. When Moses came down from the mountain that final time, the face of Moses also shined like the sun.

The Numbers Chapters Matthew 18-20

The fourth section with Matthew (18-20) corresponds to the message and theme of the book of Numbers. This begins with a famous incident in which Jesus took a little child, set him in the midst, and said:

"Except ye be converted, and become as little children, ye shall not enter into the kingdom of heaven" (Matthew 18:3).

Only the Children Enter

This event corresponds with God's chastisement of Israel in Numbers 13-14. After hearing the stories of the twelve spies, Israel rejected the opportunity to enter the Promised Land. Because of their unbelief, God determined that Israel should stay in the wilderness for 40 years and that only the children (under 20 years old) should be allowed to enter the kingdom. Only the children could enter the kingdom! That appears to be the symbolic motivation behind the statement of our Lord in Matthew 18:3.

Discipline in the Early Church

Matthew also covers the subject of discipline among believers, which corresponds with the murmuring and grumbling recorded in the book of Numbers. In like manner, Moses deals with discipline in the book of Numbers! Jesus' fourth discourse in chapter 18 is on discipleship and fellowship.

The Deuteronomy Chapters Matthew 21-28

Matthew concludes his view of the life of Christ with eight chapters—the number of new beginning. They correspond to the Mosaic book of Deuteronomy.

The Triumphal Entry

It is most remarkable that Matthew opens this portion with Christ making a grand entry into Jerusalem—offering Himself as King Messiah. That is basically what happened in the opening chapter of Deuteronomy. Joshua delivered his message that the kingdom was available, and was rejected! In Matthew, Jesus offered Himself as the one who can bring in the kingdom. Just as the people rejected Joshua, the Israelites rejected Jesus.

In Deuteronomy 1:38-39, Moses declared that the rejected Joshua would someday accomplish what that generation rejected:

> *"But Joshua the son of Nun, which standeth before thee, he shall go in thither: encourage him: for he shall cause Israel to inherit it.*
>
> *"Moreover your little ones, which ye said should be a prey, and your children, which in that day had no knowledge between good and evil, they shall go in thither, and unto them will I give it, and they shall possess it" (Deuteronomy 1:38-39).*

The Rejected Christ Will Return

In like manner, someday, the rejected Jesus will bring in the kingdom. The generation of Jesus' day rejected, but their children will enter the kingdom through Jesus Christ!

The Olivet Discourse

This fifth and final discourse given by Jesus reflects the message of Deuteronomy. It contains a series of prophecies concerning the "end of the world." Its message covers the same theme that Moses gave. For example, in Deuteronomy 18: 18, God said to Moses:

> *"I will raise them up a Prophet from among their brethren, like unto thee, and will put my words in his mouth; and he shall speak unto them all that I shall command him.*
>
> *"And it shall come to pass, that whosoever will not hearken unto my words which he shall speak in my name, I will require it of him."*

It is most unfortunate that the people rejected
Jesus. The Jews failed to hear the prophet which
God raised up as Moses predicted. We have only
to follow the history of Jerusalem's destruction
and the 2,000 year exile of the Jews to know that
God has fulfilled the words of Moses. God required it of them.

It is comforting to note, however, that God also
promised to forgive Israel during the seventh
millennium. Deuteronomy 30:5 says:

> "And the LORD thy God will bring thee into the land
> which thy fathers possessed, and thou shalt possess it;
> and he will do thee good, and multiply thee above thy
> fathers."

This is the message of hope given in Deuteronomy
and in the closing chapters of Matthew. Truly, it is
a remarkable thing that the Gospel of Matthew
follows such an amazing Torah design!

Chapter Nine

A Microcosm
of Israel

Throughout the Old Testament, Israel is regarded as a prophetic type of Jesus Christ. But since the pages of the New Testament were closed, Jesus has become a prophetic type of Israel. It is a most astounding turn of events in prophetic truth—and one which I found very interesting!

Called Out of Egypt

To begin with, Israel was an excellent allegory of Christ. For example, Hosea wrote concerning Israel:

"When Israel was a child, then I loved him, and called my son out of Egypt" (Hosea 11:1).

This is an obvious reference to Israel. Yet, Matthew used this verse as a reference to Jesus:

> "*When he arose, he took the young child and his
> mother by night, and departed into Egypt:*
> "*And was there until the death of Herod: that it might
> be fulfilled which was spoken of the Lord by the prophet,
> saying, Out of Egypt have I called my son*" (Matthew
> 2:14-15).

Both Israel and Jesus were called a *"son"* of God.
Jesus is called God's *"only begotten son"* in John
3:16. And Israel is called God's *"firstborn"* son in
Exodus 4:22. God spoke to Moses from the burning bush:

> "*And thou shalt say unto Pharaoh, Thus saith the
> LORD, Israel is my son, even my firstborn.*"

Israel, in its historic infancy, was called the
"firstborn" son of God. Symbolically, Israel became a type of Christ who is the antitype.

The Promised Seed

The promises made to Abraham concerned both
his posterity—the children of Israel—and the
Messiah. Both are called the "seed" of Abraham:

> "*For all the land which thou seest, to thee will I give
> it, and to thy seed for ever.*
> "*And I will make thy seed as the dust of the earth; so
> that if a man can number the dust of the earth, then
> shall thy seed also be numbered*" (Genesis 13:15-16).

The *"seed"* obviously refers to the twelve tribes
of Israel. Yet, in Galatians 3:16, the term *"seed"* is

made to refer to Christ:

"Now to Abraham and his seed were the promises made. He saith not, And to seeds, as of many; but as of one, And to thy seed, which is Christ" (Galatians 3:16).

Our conclusion is that the prophecy has a place for both—Israel and Jesus Christ.

A Miracle Birth

There are many comparisons which can be made between Israel and Jesus. For example, both were the product of miracle births.

Israel found its roots in Isaac, the son of Abraham. But according to all human conditions, Isaac should have never been born. At one time, Abraham had a son by Hagar, an Egyptian handmaid, in hopes of helping God fulfill His promises. But Ishmael was not the promised son.

When the time was right, the aged Sarah bore a son of her own! This was a biological impossibility! Furthermore, Abraham was too old to sire a son—but he did! Because the Lord performed a miracle for them both, Isaac's birth was a miracle birth.

So why did God allow both Abraham and Sarah to become too old to produce children before He gave them Isaac? Because Isaac's birth was a prophecy of the birth of the Messiah. The virgin birth of Christ fulfilled the typology taught in the miracle birth of Isaac.

Despised and Rejected

There is another analogy which fulfills prophetic truth. Both Israel and Jesus Christ faced hatred and rejection. Isaiah put it this way:

"He was despised and rejected of men; a man of sorrows, and acquainted with grief: and we hid as it were our faces from him; he was despised, and we esteemed him not" (Isaiah 53:3).

According to Jewish commentaries, this passage refers to the suffering of Israel. Christian theologians, however, agree with Philip, who taught the Ethiopian Eunuch that the verses referred to Christ (Acts 8:35). So who is right? Both are right!

Historical evidence proves that Israel faced the hatred of the Philistines, the Assyrians, the Babylonians, and the Romans. In fact, no nation has ever experienced the kind of hatred that Israel has had to put up with. Anti-semitism has reared its ugly head against the Jews in every generation down through the centuries.

The Jew has never been given his due respect. Most of the great inventions that have made our lives easier were produced by Jews. A Jew invented the telephone, but Alexander Graham Bell stole his secret. A Jew invented the automobile, but Henry Ford took the idea and made a fortune with it.

Every time a Jew produced something to benefit mankind, the credit was always given to a Gentile. And the name of the Jew was removed from the history books.

Moses was the greatest lawgiver in history, but you will never read his name in the history books of American schools or universities.

Solomon was the wisest man, but his wisdom is not accredited to him in American schools and universities.

The calendar used by Western Civilization is designed around a Jew, but his name cannot be spoken in America's schools and universities. The term A.D. is Latin for "in the year of our Lord" but few people know its meaning.

Jesus Becomes a Prophecy of Israel

At this point, Israel and Jesus Christ represent each other. The suffering of Israel not only represents the suffering of Christ, but the suffering Jesus went through, which lasted only a short time, has become a prophecy of the continual suffering which has plagued the Jews down through the centuries. Isaiah's description was amazingly accurate:

"He was oppressed, and he was afflicted, yet he opened not his mouth: he is brought as a lamb to the slaughter,

*and as a sheep before her shearers is dumb, so he
openeth not his mouth"* (Isaiah 53:7).

The suffering of our Lord Jesus Christ has
become a prophecy of the suffering of the Jews—
fulfilled in the death camps of Hitler's Germany.

The Jews lined up at the doors of the gas cham-
bers and entered as meekly as a lamb to the death
that awaited them.

There was little resistance to the Nazi execu-
tioners. Psalm 39:1-4 describes the holocaust that
awaited the Jews in 1939:

*"I will keep my mouth with a bridle, while the wicked
is before me.*

*"I was dumb with silence, I held my peace, even from
good; and my sorrow was stirred.*

*"My heart was hot within me, while I was musing the
fire burned: then spake I with my tongue,*

*"LORD, make me to know my end, and the measure of
my days"* (Psalm 39:1-4).

Just as our Lord stood before His accusers and
refused to speak in His defense, the Jewish people
accepted their fate at the hands of Hitler. It is an
incredible analogy!

Beginning with the suffering of Christ, the prophetic tables are turned. What happened to Jesus
now becomes a prophecy of what will happen to
Israel.

Put to Death by the Romans

Just as Jesus was put to death by the Romans, so the nation of Israel was destroyed by the Romans. In A.D. 70, a Roman army carried out the prophecy.

Jerusalem was burned and thousands were slaughtered. In A.D. 135, Hadrian and his hordes of Roman troops emptied the Promised Land of its Chosen People and scattered them to the slave markets of the world.

Israel Suffered a "Crucifixion"

Many Christian theologians, over the centuries, thought that God had destroyed the Jews for good.

The idea of replacement theology taught that Christianity forever replaced Israel as the Chosen People. But that is just not true!

Resurrection on the Third Day

Just as Jesus was resurrected on the third day, we find that Israel has also experienced a resurrection on the third day!

Hosea, the prophet who wrote that God loved Israel and called His son out of Egypt, also wrote about the resurrection of Israel:

"Come, and let us return unto the LORD: for he hath torn, and he will heal us; he hath smitten, and he will bind us up.

"After two days will he revive us: in the third day he will raise us up, and we shall live in his sight" (Hosea 6:1-2).

Not only did Hosea predict the resurrection of Israel, he noted that it would be in the *"third day."*

Theologians regard this as a prophecy of the rebirth of Israel in 1948—each day representing a thousand years. It has been about 2,000 years since the destruction of Israel.

And right on schedule, the nation was reborn—raised up to live in His sight during the coming third millennial day.

He Will Never Die Again

But the story does not end with the resurrection of Christ or the resurrection of Israel. Jesus was raised to never die again.

In like manner, Israel was given new life in 1948. Even though the Arabs would like to drive the Jew into the Mediterranean, they will never succeed. The Jew is back to stay. Israel will never die again!

Ezekiel was taken to Jerusalem, the ruined city, and shown the skeletons of the massacre that had taken place some six months earlier—when the Babylonians burned Solomon's Temple. In the valleys around Jerusalem, the bones of his countrymen lay bleached in the sun:

"And he said unto me, Son of man, can these bones live? ... Prophesy upon these bones ... Behold, I will cause breath to enter into you, and ye shall live!" (Ezekiel 37:3-5).

This predicted resurrection of Israel came to pass in 1948. But the Arabs claimed the land. Ezekiel also had something to say about that:

"Son of man, they that inhabit those wastes of the land of Israel speak, saying, Abraham was one, and he inherited the land: but we are many; the land is given us for inheritance" (Ezekiel 33:24).

But the Arabs are in for a surprise. They do not own the Promised Land. Though the Moslems maintain a presence on the Temple Mount in Jerusalem, they will eventually have to give it up. Israel will gain its long-awaited kingdom—perhaps in the near future!

After Israel's confrontation with the antichrist and the rest of the world, Christ will return—just as Israel returned!

Jesus Christ will fulfill His prophetic promises and set up the kingdom of heaven. He will rule the entire world from Jerusalem for a thousand years. You can count on it! Why? Because what happened to Israel also happened to Jesus. And what happened to Jesus is also happening to Israel. What a blessed future lies ahead!

To recap, there are several things that happened to both Israel and Jesus:

1. Both are called the son of God.
2. Both births were miracles.
3. Both went into Egypt.
4. Both were despised and rejected.
5. Both were put to death by the Romans.
6. Both were raised on the third day.
7. Neither will ever—ever—ever die again!

In the days of the Old Testament, Israel was a microcosm of Christ. But since the days of the New Testament, Christ has become a microcosm of Israel.

Chapter Ten

The Covenant of Abraham

The single most difficult problem which has faced Christian theologians down through the centuries has been the subject of "salvation by grace" versus "salvation by the works of the Law." The subject has divided theologians in every generation.

Paul wrote extensively about the subject. He was constantly plagued with Judaizers who contended that his Gentile converts should be circumcised and keep the law of Moses. Paul maintained that Gentiles were saved by faith and faith alone. On the other hand, James wrote, "*... show me thy faith without thy works, and I will show thee my faith by my works*" (James 2:18).

This argument has kept heads spinning down through the centuries! Peter was a devout Jew

who reluctantly carried the Gospel to a Gentile—
the Roman centurion, Cornelius. Peter said of
Paul's writings:

> "And account that the long-suffering of our Lord is
> salvation; even as our beloved brother Paul also accord-
> ing to the wisdom given unto him hath written unto you;
>   As also in all his epistles, speaking in them of these
> things; in which are some things hard to be understood..."
> (II Peter 3:15-16).

Peter had a difficult time understanding so
complex a matter. Furthermore, in his first epistle,
Peter said that even the angels had a bit of
difficulty with this part of God's plan:

> "Unto whom it was revealed, that not unto them-
> selves, but unto us they did minister the things, which
> are now reported unto you by them that have preached
> the gospel unto you with the Holy Ghost sent down from
> heaven; which things the angels desire to look into"
> (I Peter 1:12).

Even the angels cannot comprehend the grace
God has bestowed upon us! If Peter confessed to
having a hard time understanding, and reported
that even the angels desired to look into the
matter, no wonder Christianity has been in a
quandary down through the centuries! From this
difficulty has arisen over a thousand differing
denominations—most of them built around a particular view of what constitutes salvation.

The difficulty seems to have resulted from

Israel's view of the Mosaic Law. Early Christianity was born out of a culture that circumcised every male child. Each family strictly observed the Jewish festivals—Passover, Pentecost, Trumpets, the Day of Atonement, and Tabernacles. In fact, the society rigidly kept 613 laws of Moses which governed every area of their lives. They even worshiped on Saturday!

Theologians normally think of salvation by grace as saving us from these difficult laws. They think that Jesus nailed the Mosaic Law to the cross—that He fulfilled the Law and therefore did away with it.

On the other hand, some Gentile Christians in our day want us to return to a keeping of Jewish ritual. Messianic congregations are filled with Gentiles who meet on Friday nights. They eat kosher foods and observe as many of the 613 Mosaic laws as they possibly can. Another Christian denomination worships on Saturday and urges their people to observe their stylized version of the Mosaic Law.

Some Jewish believers in *Yeshua Ha Meshiach* (Jesus the Messiah) preach that the Jesus worshiped by most Christian denominations today is not the same Jesus of the New Testament. They claim that the Jesus we serve is a Gentile concoction that doesn't even resemble the original Jesus

of Nazareth. I've read one Messianic Jewish believer in *Yeshua* who claims we are all idolaters
and that *Yeshua* (Jesus) will throw us all into hell
when He comes! The argument rages on!

It is true that Law versus Grace is a deep and
difficult concept to comprehend, much less explain. However, perhaps we can help put the
problem into a proper perspective. Let me start by
saying that the Law of Moses never offered eternal life in the first place. Surprised? Allow me to
explain.

Before there was a Moses, there was a man
named Abraham. Before there was a Mosaic Covenant, there was an Abrahamic Covenant that
offered eternal life!

Don't miss the importance of this. The entire
New Testament is related to the Abrahamic Covenant. The New Testament is not related to the
Old Testament Mosaic Law in the matter of eternal life.

I must admit, for most of my life I thought it
was. I thought the New Testament replaced the
Mosaic Law. I was wrong. The New Testament
doctrine of salvation by grace is not related to the
Law of Moses. That is what the Apostle Paul was
driving at in his epistles to the Romans and
Galatians. That is the message in the treatise to
the Hebrews.

These controversial passages were actually Paul's explanation to a Jewish culture that their salvation was not dependent upon the Mosaic Covenant after all, but rather upon the Abrahamic Covenant!

When the New Testament was written, Matthew introduced the entire subject of eternal life through Jesus Christ by announcing that He was the *"son of David"* and the *"son of Abraham."* There was no mention about Moses or his Law.

Jesus is the fulfillment of the Abrahamic Covenant and the Davidic Covenant. The covenant made with David was an extension of the covenant made with Abraham. It offered the same promises.

Matthew's genealogy of Christ begins with Abraham. Matthew does not carry the genealogy back to Adam, as does Luke, because the subject of eternal life by grace through faith goes back to Abraham.

The first five books of the Bible (Genesis through Deuteronomy) are generally considered to be the Mosaic Law. But, if you review the first five books carefully, you will note that the Mosaic Law was introduced in Exodus—not Genesis.

Genesis introduces, not the Mosaic Covenant but, the Covenant of Abraham. And that is the covenant upon which even the Jews base their concept of eternal life.

When a Jew prays, he prays to the God of Abraham—not in the name of Moses. Christians close prayers in the name of Jesus.

When a Jew died in Bible days, he went to Abraham's bosom—not Moses' bosom. Paradise was placed in the charge of Abraham—not Moses. The very name of heaven comes from the site of the tomb of Abraham, Isaac, and Jacob. Abraham bought a cave at Hebron, which means, "seat of association." Genesis 23:19 says:

> *"And after this, Abraham buried Sarah his wife in the cave of the field of Machpelah before Mamre: the same is Hebron in the land of Canaan"* (Genesis 23:19).

Again, Genesis 25:10 says:

> *"The field which Abraham purchased of the sons of Heth: there was Abraham buried, and Sarah his wife"* (Genesis 25:10).

Hebron became the capital of Israel under David for the first seven years of his reign. David then moved the capital to Jerusalem. Hebron, from which comes the name of heaven, was a "seat of association" until the kingdom was moved to Jerusalem. In like manner, the bosom of Abraham is associated with the future eternal city, New Jerusalem.

In Matthew 8:5-13, the story is given of a Gentile who came to Jesus seeking healing for his servant. The Gentile was a Roman centurion. When Jesus told him that He would come and heal his servant, the Gentile said:

"I am not worthy that thou shouldest come under my roof: but speak the word only, and my servant shall be healed" (v. 8).

When Jesus heard the Gentile make such a statement, he said:

"I have not found so great faith, no, not in Israel" (v. 10).

The next statement is based, not on the Mosaic Covenant but, upon the Abrahamic Covenant. Keep in mind, this Gentile exhibited *"great faith,"* having never kept the Law of Moses. Jesus made this startling statement:

"I say unto you, That many [Gentiles] *shall come from the east and west, and shall sit down with Abraham, and Isaac, and Jacob, in the kingdom of heaven"* (v. 11).

There is no mention here of Moses. The kingdom of heaven is based upon the covenant made with Abraham and passed on through his posterity—Isaac, Jacob, etc. Yes, Moses will be in the kingdom of heaven, but not because of his Law. Moses will be there because he believed in the Abrahamic Covenant! And so will Samuel, and Isaiah, and Jeremiah, and Daniel, and Jonah, and Ezekiel, and all the rest!

Jesus included Gentiles *"from the east and west"* who will join Abraham in the kingdom of heaven. Those Gentiles will not get there because they adopted or kept the Mosaic ordinances.

They will get there by trusting in that part of the Abrahamic Covenant which promised, *"God will provide himself a **Lamb**!"* (Genesis 22:8).

When we arrive at the very conclusion of the New Testament, we will find that *"The Revelation of Jesus Christ"* reveals Him as that *Lamb*! John writes:

> *"And I beheld, and, lo, in the midst of the throne and of the four beasts, and in the midst of the elders, stood a **Lamb** as it had been slain ..."* (Revelation 5:6).

Look around the throne room. Do you see a reference to the Mosaic Covenant? No. Throughout the entire book of Revelation there is only one mention of Moses. And the reference is to the Song of Moses, not his Law (Revelation 15:3).

In the final chapters of Revelation, Christ is portrayed over and over again as the **Lamb**.

The holy city New Jerusalem belongs to the Lamb! John is taken to see the **"Lamb's** *wife*!" (Revelation 21:9). On the foundation of the city are written the names of the *"twelve apostles of the **Lamb**"* (v. 14). The city needs no sun or moon to shine in it for *"the **Lamb** is the light thereof"* (v. 23). Those who live there have their names written in the *"**Lamb's** book of life"* (v. 27). The *"throne of God and of the **Lamb** shall be in it"* (Revelation 22:3).

This is the Lamb of the Abrahamic Covenant. It was Abraham who *"looked for a city which hath foundations, whose builder and maker is God"* (Hebrews 11:10).

This amazing statement about the faith of Abraham is the key to understanding the concept of eternal life. The faith of Abraham is the foundation upon which the doctrine of eternal life in the New Testament is written.

When Jesus died on Calvary, he made the faith of Abraham available to all—including Gentiles. Besides, the Jews were never saved by the works of the Law in the first place! They based their hope of eternal life by faith in the promises made to Abraham!

Of course, by the first century, many Jews were so steeped in the Mosaic Law that they could not understand the message of salvation by faith in the promises of Abraham.

John 9:28 points up the problem: *"Then they reviled him, and said, Thou art his disciple; but we are Moses' disciples."* They based their hope of eternal life on the Mosaic Law instead of on the faith of Abraham.

Earlier, Jesus had explained their problem. In John 7:19, Jesus said, *"Did not Moses give you the law, and yet none of you keepeth the law?"* The Law could not save, because it is impossible to keep. Only Jesus kept it perfectly.

In Acts 3, Peter addressed the Jews after healing the lame man at the gate of the temple. He began his sermon by saying:

> *"The God of Abraham, and of Isaac, and of Jacob, the God of our fathers, hath glorified his Son Jesus ..."* (Acts 3:13).

He did not refer to the God of Moses. He turned the attention of the people to the very basis of their hope for eternal life. He talked about the God of Abraham!

When Stephen addressed the Sanhedrin, he opened his sermon with Abraham's encounter with God:

> *"Men, brethren, and fathers, hearken: The God of glory appeared unto our father Abraham ..."* (Acts 7:2).

Stephen began with the very foundation of their faith—the Covenant of Abraham.

When Paul preached his first recorded sermon at Antioch of Pisidia, he addressed the people as,

"Men and brethren, children of the stock of Abraham ..." (Acts 13:26). Paul's message took the people back to the very foundation of their faith—Abraham.

The epistle to the Romans was written to explain to the Jews at Rome that their loyalty to the Law of Moses was not then, nor ever had been, the basis for their hope of eternal life. He showed that the Law existed for the sole purpose of exposing their sins. The Law offered only a curse.

When Paul illustrated the basis of eternal life, he used the faith of Abraham to do it. In chapter 4, Paul showed how Abraham was saved by faith long before there was a law. In fact, Abraham was saved by faith even long before he was circumcised:

> *"What shall we say then that Abraham our father, as pertaining to the flesh, hath found?*
> *"For if Abraham were justified by works, he hath whereof to glory; but not before God.*
> *"For what saith the scripture? Abraham believed God, and it was counted unto him for righteousness"* (Romans 4:1-3).

To show that the promises God made to Abraham were not based upon the Mosaic Law, uncircumcised Gentiles were included in it:

> *"Cometh this blessedness then upon the circumcision only, or upon the uncircumcision also? for we say that faith was reckoned to Abraham for righteousness"* (Romans 4:9).

Not only was Abraham the father of Judaism, but of Gentile Christianity as well:

"And the father of circumcision to them who are not of the circumcision only, but who also walk in the steps of that faith of our father Abraham, which he had being yet uncircumcised" (Romans 4:12).

The basis for the entire doctrine of eternal life was not based upon Moses, but Abraham. Paul put it this way in Romans 4:13:

"For the promise, that he should be the heir of the world, was not to Abraham, or to his seed, through the law, but through the righteousness of faith" (Romans 4:13).

The Covenant with Abraham was extended to Gentiles because that was one of the main goals of the Covenant to begin with.

In Genesis 22:18, the Gentiles were included in the Covenant of Abraham:

"And in thy seed shall all the nations of the earth be blessed; because thou hast obeyed my voice" (Genesis 22:18).

Again, in Genesis 26:4, the same promise is given:

"And I will make thy seed to multiply as the stars of heaven, and will give unto thy seed all these countries; and in thy seed shall all the nations of the earth be blessed" (Genesis 26:4).

The Covenant of Abraham is the prevailing

covenant—not the Covenant of Moses. In Galatians 3:13-14, Paul was quite clear concerning our basis for eternal life:

"Christ hath redeemed us from the curse of the law ...
"That the blessing of Abraham might come on the Gentiles through Jesus Christ; that we might receive the promise of the Spirit through faith" (Galatians 3:13-14).

Note that Paul refers to the Law of Moses as a condemning factor, not a saving factor. He called it *"the curse of the law."* That was the purpose of the Law from the beginning. It revealed the curse of sin, yet had no method for relief. The Law and its sacrifices all pointed to Christ—the only redeeming factor—and Christ offers eternal life through the Abrahamic Covenant, not the Mosaic Covenant.

Furthermore, Paul says that no one can ever—ever—ever annul the Abrahamic Covenant. It is still active to this very day!

"Brethren, I speak after the manner of men; Though it be but a man's covenant, yet if it be confirmed, no man disannulleth, or addeth thereto.
"Now to Abraham and his seed were the promises made" (Galatians 3:15-16).

The Order of Melchizedek

We are told in Hebrews that Christ is a High Priest after the order of Melchizedek, unto whom Abraham paid tithes. Melchizedek was a priest who lived in the days of Abraham, not Moses.

Furthermore, even Levi (father of the Levitical priesthood under the Mosaic Law) paid tithes to Melchizedek:

> "And as I may so say, Levi also, who receiveth tithes, paid tithes in Abraham.
> "For he was yet in the loins of his father, when Melchizedek met him" (Hebrews 7:9-10).

According to the treatise to the Hebrews, Christ is not related to the Levitical priesthood under the Mosaic Law, but to the Melchizedek priesthood and the Covenant of Abraham.

The Schoolmaster

Now, let's consider the unique purpose of the Mosaic Law. In Galatians 3:24, the Law of Moses is introduced as a schoolmaster:

> "Wherefore the law was our schoolmaster to bring us unto Christ, that we might be justified by faith" (Galatians 3:24).

The work of *"schoolmaster"* allows us to detect a Torah design throughout the pages of the New Testament. For example: Matthew divides the life of Christ into five parts, corresponding to the themes found in Genesis, Exodus, Leviticus, Numbers, and Deuteronomy. This framework for the Gospel shows the *"schoolmaster"* or teaching aspect of the Mosaic Law seen in the Divine design.

The Seven Lamps of the Mosaic Menorah can

be seen throughout the New Testament—especially in the Book of Revelation. Why? Because the Law is a teacher or *"schoolmaster."* The intricate design work of Almighty God can be seen through the Mosaic Law. Proof that the Bible could only have been written by an all-knowing God can be seen in its Torah designs. That is the purpose of the Mosaic Law. It is a teaching mechanism to prove the Divine handiwork of God.

The Tabernacle, Jewish prayer shawl, the Priesthood, its liturgy, etc., offer magnificent views of the glory of our faith. But those things are just teachers (schoolmasters) to point us to faith in Christ. They are not the basis of salvation. Only faith in the **Lamb** promised to Abraham can bring eternal life.